CHRISTIANITY WITHOUT DOGMA

A Personalized Way to Deconstruct Christian Beliefs and Practices

By Jack Bergstrand

Table of Contents

Preface

THE FUTURE OF Christianity resides in the hearts and minds of young people. Things could look better than they currently do. Prayer, church attendance, and belief in God and doctrine have declined with each generation. In the latest Pew Research report on this subject:

- Only 38% of Millennials (people born between 1981 and 1997) feel that religion is "very important" to their lives;
- More than twice as many 18–29-year-olds are sure there is not a God (38%) as who are sure there is (18%);
- The most common religious identity among Americans ages 18 to 29 is *none*.

We will probably never know for sure how much of this decline is due to unprovable theology-based dogma or tangential issues such as the dogmatically intense Christian Nationalism movement. But regardless of the reasons, Christianity's declines aren't only about the numbers anyway. Behind these statistics, there are suffering people. Many have experienced significant personal trauma from Christian churches, including being hurt by misogynistic practices and purity culture, marginalized as black, indigenous, and people of color, and shamed and silenced as non-heterosexuals. The abuse has been sustained through chauvinistic religious cultures that are and have always been dominated by straight, white, conservative Christian males.

The declines in Christianity are corroborated through many sources. According to research conducted by the Deconstruction Network, the deconstruction movement, comprised of people actively questioning their previously held core religious beliefs, is today's fastest-growing spiritual group. Every day, 2,700 people leave the American church, yet 78% wish to keep some aspect of the faith they are leaving. Despite declines in religious affiliation, spirituality has increased by 14% for the religious and non-religious alike.

The Christian deconstruction community has been growing through various groups, including Exvangelicals, the Deconstruction Network, the New Evangelicals, Decolonizing Theology, God is Grey, Naked Pastor, Deconstructing Purity Culture, Straight White American Jesus, and Dirty Rotten Church Kids, to name a few. Members are active on social media and unafraid to publicly disagree with Christian practices that have been unquestioned—and even legally protected—over the centuries.

Deconstruction seems to be hurting Christian churches in two ways. Beyond the steady membership declines, churches are contracting and radicalizing. As more moderate Christians continue to leave, the remaining leaders and congregational members seem increasingly inclined to double down and become even more extreme in their commitment to their theologies and social and political stances.

Whatever their motivations for leaving, deconstruction is often difficult for those who are deconstructing. People have been traumatized, found it necessary to challenge many of their deepest beliefs, been shunned by friends and families, and found no viable options other than disconnecting from the religious and social support systems that have sustained them throughout their lives. *Christianity Without Dogma* was written with this backdrop in mind.

Beginning with defining the words used in the book's title, *Christianity* is defined as the Christian religion overall. While the faith has many flavors, each professes to follow Jesus Christ and the teachings of the Bible. Second, *dogma* is defined as a religious belief that is not provable by outside parties and is positioned as unquestionably true by organizational leaders. Christianity without dogma, in combination, is an alternative way to think about the Christian faith, where people can feel safe following Jesus without needing to believe unprovable things. It tries to build deconstruction into the faith itself.

This book is for people who are rethinking their Christian beliefs, whether in public or in private. It is written to help people examine their faith, become better able to explain their situation to other Christians using biblical language, and hopefully grow spiritually as part of the process. Throughout the book, the mindset is that deconstruction is not bad and is needed for Christians to grow. Deconstructing Christians are in good company indeed: Jesus himself helped to deconstruct the Jewish religion, with love fulfilling the law.

The deconstruction movement, comprised of people actively questioning their previously held core religious beliefs, is today's fastest-growing spiritual group. Christians have become trapped in a dogmatic cage of Christianity, Inc.'s own making, but that cage can be unlocked through deconstructing the system that built and maintains it. As I peeled away unprovable Christian dogma in my own life, it became clear that dogma had more to do with the business of Christianity than the purpose of Christianity.

In this book, I deconstruct Christianity through the lens of what Jesus prioritized as most important: love, connection, and service. Although I recognize that the Bible is a source of significant trauma for many deconstructing Christians, I have included many linkages to scripture. If you have been traumatized by Christians who have weaponized the Bible at your expense, I hope you will stick with me. I promise it will be used carefully and lovingly.

Christianity is in trouble. When I cover the stages of decline in Chapter 8, this will become clearer. Christianity has unfortunately become the faith of our fathers instead of a faith for our children. In the process, while preaching hate and calling it love, dogmatic churches, have become increasingly political and hostile to those outside of their sanctuaries. They have become trapped in a dogmatic cage of Christianity, Inc.'s own making, but that cage can be unlocked through deconstructing the system that has built and maintained it.

This book was not written for people who earn their livings from the faith or who believe that Christianity is fine just the way it is. It's not because paid theologians and church employees are bad people, but they are not in great positions to fix the system they are employed to defend. A more independent and objective assessment is needed, and this book provides a perspective outside of any Christian organization's reach or endorsement.

Despite the problems associated with Christianity's decline, the faith's organizational strength remains impressive. More than 2.3 billion people identify as Christians globally. In the United States alone, there are more than 300,000 churches and more than 200 Christian denominations. Given that there are only 14,000 McDonald's restaurants in the US, the sheer number of churches in existence is stunning.

*   *   *

As for me, while I am not associated with a Christian organization and am not an important part of the deconstruction movement, I am a deconstructed evangelical. I grew up in a loving and stable evangelical family in a small town a half-century ago. While I was taught a lot of dogma growing up, and some of the systems of oppression were already in place, Christianity seemed a little kinder and gentler back then, and it was certainly less politically militant. As I got older, I stayed evangelical at heart but found that a lot of what was considered spiritual but not religious seemed more Jesus-like than what organized churches were offering. It seemed less judgmental, more loving, and much more contemplative.

Over several decades, I dedicated much of my time to business, education, and helping to raise a family, but I committed to myself that I would one day try to synthesize my thoughts on the Bible, what I had been taught growing up, experience with spiritual contemplation, and what I believed a more honest Christian practice could look like. I thought Christianity could be kinder, more loving, intellectually honest, welcoming to others, and contemplative. You know, more like Jesus.

On my journey, I deconstructed in a very rigorous way over the past decade, which resulted in me writing this book. During this time, I found that while Jesus' priorities of love, non-judgment, forgiveness, and helping others were consistent with being spiritual but not religious, fundamentalist dogma was not. No matter how many mental gymnastics I went through, harmonizing Jesus' priorities and spiritual consciousness with church doctrine and how the Bible was used by many hateful Christian leaders was a futile exercise. The core issues that I found revolved around a system of unconscious duality, religion instead of spirituality, dogma as a product, corrupt organizational hierarchies, and nonsensical conceptualizations of God. A chapter is dedicated to each of these interdependencies.

When writing this book, I tried to stay intellectually honest and curious. As I deconstructed Christian dogma and examined the system that produced it, it became increasingly clear that dogma had more to do with the business of Christianity than the priorities of Jesus. I appreciate that this may seem unfair to some in that there is a common belief that dogma (or doctrine or authoritative teaching about God, Jesus, Spirit, Bible, church, etc.) is simply an effort for groups to systematize what they consider important. For me, the Christianity that emerged was one increasingly distilled into Jesus' priorities of *Love, Connection, and Service*.

While deconstructing, I ended up shedding unprovable dogma, expecting to reintroduce some of it later. But to my surprise, once the dogma was removed, I found that I didn't need to reintroduce it. For me, dogma turned out to be like training wheels on a bike. It helped me to get started with Christianity when I was young but eventually kept me from going full speed as I got older.

* * *

Christianity Without Dogma is not an attack on Christianity. Neither is it a post-modernist rant or an effort to cancel out the ghosts of Christianity's past. Instead, it was written to try to help deconstructing

Christians reflect more deeply on their Christian practices in a more systematic and honest way. The book is for those who love or at one point loved being a Christian but no longer like what Christianity has become, have grown beyond their childhood belief systems, feel spiritually suffocated, have been religiously traumatized, or have experienced some combination of these things.

Throughout this book, there will be a variety of Christian choices. I hope those who are spiritual but not religious, those who find rationalism empty, and those who wish they did not have to abandon the good parts of their Christian faith because of the bad parts of the Christian business model can all find something useful. My goal for *Christianity Without Dogma* is to help deconstructing Christians create their own best paths forward.

PREFACE SUMMARY IN STORYBOOK FORM:

- Once upon a time, Christians believed that their religious dogma was the foundation of their faith.
- Every day, they argued about their dogma and separated from one another because of it.
- One day, Christians began to ask what it would be like if they no longer argued about dogma.
- Because of that, they decided to embrace what Jesus said was most important and turned love into their Christian compass.
- Because of that, unprovable dogma stopped being a thing.
- Until finally, they became more like Jesus.
- And then they were able to live happily ever after.

1

The Breaking Cross

They will beat their swords into plowshares and their spears into pruning hooks. Nation will not take up sword against nation, nor will they train for war anymore.

Isaiah 2:4, NIV

CHRISTIANITY IS DYING a death of a thousand cuts and Christian leaders seem to be the ones doing the cutting. As churches continue to lose their spiritual relevance with members and moral authority with people outside the faith, young people are rejecting the faith *en masse* and older Christians also seem to be increasingly losing interest. To explore why, this chapter assesses the Christian landscape through the lens of an independent consultant. It highlights key parts of the business system of Christianity that can help us understand how and why the Christian machine works the way it does. Each part is described in subsequent chapters to explain the faith as a system. With a new perspective on and a better understanding of this system, those who are deconstructing may be able to move forward with greater clarity and confidence. This chapter aims to help deconstructing Christians understand how to turn Christianity's dogmatic swords into plow-shares and its spears into pruning hooks.

* * *

Millions of people watched in shock as an overwhelmingly white male right-wing group of insurgents and conspiracy theorists stormed the United States Capitol on January 6, 2021. A cacophony of raised banners flew. Some proclaimed *Keep America Great*, US flags flew along-side Confederate, and both were used as clubs against law enforcement officers. Acting on statements by the President himself, white suprem-acists and other militant Americans stood in battle gear, some literally foaming at their mouths as they cried out, "Stop the steal!"

What could be worse?

For many Christians, there was indeed something worse. It was seeing "Jesus" banners and banners proclaiming *Jesus Saves* waving in the air right alongside racially, religiously, and politically hateful slogans. Was this all just a big misunderstanding? Were these Christian brothers and sisters simply confused, thinking that the Capitol was about to host a Sean Feucht worship concert for Jesus? Alas, there was no confusion. Politically radicalized Christians had been cultivated in and called to action from churches that had increasingly been con-verted into terrorist sleeper cells.

Only two months later, in Atlanta, Georgia, a 21-year-old Christian took it upon himself to kill eight people, most of them Asian women, because of Christian guilt about his sexual impulses. During the same period, it was revealed (after his death) that Ravi Zacharias, one of fundamentalist Christianity's most prominent apologists, had lived a secret life of sexual abuse, including having his own network of day spas. Further highlighting a long history of Christian criminality, a few months after the Atlanta killings, more than 200 unmarked graves filled with the skeletons of more than 1,000 children as young as three years old were discovered in Canada, where Catholic boarding schools had attempted to assimilate Indigenous children and convert them to Christianity from 1900 to 1971.

(Is Christianity, a faith where Jesus prioritized loving God and others, non-judgment, continuous forgiveness, and unselfish service to those in need, doomed?)

After the September 11, 2001 attacks, Christian pundits questioned why prominent Islamic leaders did not forcefully speak out against the carnage that radical Islamic terrorists caused after flying commercial airliners into buildings full of people. Yet two decades later, prominent right-wing Christian leaders also failed to speak up in a forceful and organized way about similar underlying issues with the Christian faith. If anything, radicalized Christians and right-wing media personalities doubled down on hateful and disingenuous positions. How could this happen? It is admittedly hard to condemn one's own religion. Religions are complex psychologically, sociologically, and historically, have many fear-based ingredients, and possess a wide range of loosely related and emotionally charged practices and ideologies. No one person or group has the official standing to speak for the Christian religion overall. The Pope can speak for Catholics, but even that authority is not easy to exert. And there are large numbers of Protestants who don't consider Catholics to be Christians, anyway.

It's complicated.

Was storming the Capitol a big misunderstanding, or had politically radicalized Christians been cultivated in and called to action from churches that had increasingly been turned into terrorist sleeper cells? Has Christianity entered into a death spiral? Can it be saved? Are the declines happening despite Christian dogma or because of it?

Christian right-wing extremism is increasing the momentum of the deconstruction movement. Christianity itself, which began as a faith based on Jesus' messages of love and reconciliation, appears to have gone to the dark side. In some churches, it's as if Jesus has become the honorary chairman of the National Rifle Association. Has Christianity entered into a death spiral? Can it be saved? Is all of this happening *despite* Christian dogma or *because* of it? Is this simply a problem of radical Christian fundamentalism, with old white men yearning to go back to a time that never existed, or are Christianity's troubles symptomatic of larger systemic problems?

CHRISTIANITY THROUGH THE EYES OF A BUSINESS TRANSFORMATION CONSULTANT

Typically, a theologian or minister would write a book on Christian deconstruction, or perhaps a well-known voice in the deconstruction space. I am none of these, which is an advantage in this case. For more than 20 years, I have been a business transformation consultant helping executives of large public companies. During the 20 years prior to that, I was an executive for one of the oldest and largest companies in the world, Coca-Cola. What could a business transformation consultant and business executive possibly add to the Christian deconstruction conversation? One of the reasons I'm adding my voice to the current conversation is that I don't believe that some of Christianity's problems are the types of issues that can be productively solved by theologians and ministers, especially those who are already personally invested in the Christian system. An independent examination of the faith's underlying system is needed to help explain many of the troubling symptoms that have become painfully obvious.

Many readers are probably not familiar with what independent consultants do. In a nutshell, consultants diagnose and try to help organizations adjust to changing environments. They ask questions such as the following:

- What are the root causes of specific problems?
- How do the systemic pieces fit together?
- What is working, not working, and why?
- What is the goal, and what is getting in the way of the goal?
- What are the available options?
- What are the recommendations?

The role of an independent consultant is different from the role of a theologian or clergy member. To make a comparison to the business world, consider that academics study and teach at universities, managers work in companies, and consultants bridge these two groups. In Christianity, theologians are like academics in seminaries, and ministers are like managers in churches. Compared to the academic and manager roles, consultants take a *bigger picture* view than managers and a more *operational* view than academics. Since consultants are independent, they are in a better position to help clients see past their blind spots and help them to examine things that they were previously unable or unwilling to question.

Interactions between academics, managers, and consultants are not always harmonious. For example, theologians and ministers may react to this book like academics and practitioners sometimes react to business consultants. As I use the Bible to support an alternative Christian model, theologians may argue that how I use theology lacks nuance or is even flat-out wrong versus their formal training. Likewise, ministers might argue that someone who is not part of the clergy, or even a church member for that matter, has no credibility. Consultants do sometimes hear these types of arguments more generally. However, the advantage of an independent consultant's perspective is that it is sometimes more important and beneficial to focus on how things could work better than it is to be an expert on the inner workings of a current state that is failing.

Consultants want their clients to improve and are engaged to tell leaders what they might not want to hear. They truly care about their clients and want them to succeed. They do not attack; rather, they probe and try to act as catalysts for change. Importantly, consultants are not the ultimate decision-makers. Eventually, it is up to the client to accept or reject the consultant's recommendations. In this book, I will look at the Christian system in an independent way, first through the personal lens of an individual who is deconstructing and then through an operational lens for deconstructing churches more generally.

THE MULTI-FACETED CHRISTIAN LANDSCAPE

When you grow up in a church, it can be easy to think about Christianity in the narrow terms you were taught. Christianity is not monolithic, however. There are many types of churches, and while this book focuses mostly on larger and higher-profile ones, the average church is small. Most have less than 75 members, and despite some exceptions, most Christian ministers earn modest incomes. Clergy also have relatively limited employment options outside of their denominational belief systems. While in principle, there is one Christian church and one body of Christ, in practice, organizations compete with one another for members. Churches are like other businesses in this sense, and this helps explain why there are hundreds of different Christian denominations in the United States and around the world.

DECONSTRUCTING IN REAL LIFE: *"I am a recovering evangelical Christian for many reasons. For example, our pastor sent out an email to the congregation that he didn't believe that wearing masks was right because they covered our faces and we were to be the image-bearers of God. The Bible was used to make me feel minuscule as a woman, and I was told not to associate with my half-brother because he was gay. I took Christianity very seriously, but at the time of the Trump election, I could no longer be associated with a group that was so hateful, ignorant, and close-minded."*

Understanding the competitive nature of Christian churches is important during the deconstruction process because people typically deconstruct in reaction to their own church's teachings, and different Christian factions use the Bible and dogma differently. Some churches emphasize Bible-based love and forgiveness, while others picket in the streets with hateful slogans as egregious as "God hates fags." Within the four walls of an individual church, Christianity is often claimed to be a simple faith (often with the idea of one true way). However, it is quite complicated across churches and the broader Christian ecosystem.

When people say they are *Christians*, what they mean can vary greatly, even inside specific churches. It is like saying that every American is the same, or that every person in your company or family is just like every other. Even once someone has committed to be a Catholic or Protestant, or a Baptist or Lutheran, he or she will find many variances across their own church's members. Consider, for example, a few church-affiliation archetypes that are outlined in Table 1.1. Differences like these inside churches affect how people view their faith and influence personal deconstruction processes. For example, fundamentalist Christians who become atheists are often pre-wired to become fundamentalist atheists.

Table 1.1. Church-Affiliation Archetypes

ARCHETYPE	DEFINITION	IMPLICATION
Fundamentalists	Firm believers of all their church's dogma	To not believe one part of the dogma is to not believe any of it
Moderates	Doubt some dogma but can live with what they still believe	Determine that it is easier to go along than to leave
Socialites	Do not care about the dogma and enjoy the fellowship	The church is like a club membership

Within churches, ministers are trained and paid to teach and defend their denomination's dogma. Even though Christian dogma is often seen as the foundation of the faith, it is more accurate to describe it as the byproduct of the church's denominational business system. When deconstructing Christian dogma, before someone can truly know *what* they believe, it's helpful to understand *why* they were taught to believe it in the first place. Looking at the faith like a business system can help Christians deconstruct more easily and avoid getting stuck in morasses of incompatible dogmatic arguments without straightforward ways to navigate out.

This book looks at Christianity as a system through a series of spiritual, rational, and religious lenses linked to the Bible in a non-theological, Jesus-centric way. To do this, I reviewed the faith from three angles. One perspective was to look at what a Bible-based *spiritual but not religious* form of Christianity might look like. A second perspective was to look at the faith through a *rational* lens. Finally, I looked at Christianity through the fundamentalist lens I had learned growing up. Once this review through these varying perspectives was complete, an underlying system of five interdependencies became apparent.

FIVE CHRISTIAN INTERDEPENDENCIES

After examining Christianity as a system, five interdependencies emerged:

- Consciousness,
- Religion,
- Dogma,
- Organizations, and
- the Godhead.

These interdependencies all influence the way Christianity works as a system, and they can be used to help inform one's deconstruction process. While they often influence one another, it is easier to first look at them sequentially. For example, understanding *consciousness* through a Christian lens makes it easier to deconstruct Christianity as a *religion*. Understanding Christianity as a *religion* can help one better understand how *dogma* is used as a Christian platform, and understanding *dogma* as a platform is connected to how Christian *organizations* operate. With these interdependencies established, it is easier to understand how Christians define the nature of *God*. Each of the five Christian interdependencies is important, but ultimately, the interactions between them make the Christian system act the way it does. By first understanding these interdependencies as a system, I believe that many deconstructing Christians will be able to chart their own courses with greater clarity and less trauma.

Figure 1.1. Five Systemic Christian Interdependencies

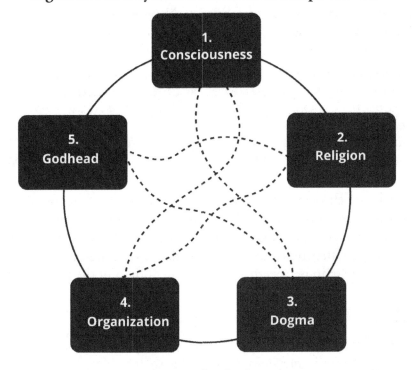

Dogma is often a trigger point that leads to deconstruction. Yet, it is typically not the best place to start because dogma is usually a byproduct of the larger Christian system that has created and sustained it. This interdependence between dogma and system makes it hard for deconstructing Christians to get useful answers to their theological questions from church leaders. The system won't allow it. By taking on a holistic view of the Christian business system, deconstructing Christians may find it easier to assess their personal situations and make better choices.

Deconstructing Christians have increasingly opted out of the system as fundamentalists have chosen to turn their plowshares into swords and pruning hooks into spears. If these trends continue, more churches will struggle to survive. Moreover, North America, like Europe before it, looks to be heading toward becoming post-Christian. In 2021, according to the New York Times, about 26% of Americans identified as having no religious affiliation, but only two-tenths of one percent of Congressional members identified this way.[1] Therefore, despite the best efforts of Christian Nationalists, the probabilities favor greater political secularization in the future.

> **DECONSTRUCTING IN REAL LIFE:** *"Christian theology made me too afraid to live and too afraid to die. I needed to begin the deconstruction journey to break free from the toxicity. I have put behind me the cruelty, abuse, and shame of the church and what religion has misrepresented God to be. For the first time in my life, I am at a place where I feel permission to be alive. The abuse had to stop."*

A better choice for Christians is to embrace deconstruction, experience greater levels of spiritual growth, and serve more people in need, one person and one congregation at a time. To do this, the first interdependency that needs to be examined is the nature of *consciousness* from a Christian perspective, which is the subject of the next chapter.

CHAPTER SUMMARY IN STORYBOOK FORM

- Once upon a time, Christians did not question what their religious leaders told them to believe.
- Every day, they joined churches and faithfully pledged allegiance to their congregation's particular denominational business model.
- One day, members began discussing the problems they had with Christian dogma and discovered that deconstruction could make them better Christians.
- Because of that, they discovered that deconstruction could help the entire Christian system.
- Because of that, more Christians began to wake up spiritually.
- Until finally, Christianity became more like Jesus—more loving, connecting, and serving.
- And then they were able to live happily ever after.

---

[1] Ryan Burge, "A More Secular America Is Not Just a Problem for Republicans," The New York Times (*The New York Times*, August 25, 2021), https://www.nytimes.com/2021/08/25/opinion/republicans-democrats-america-religion.html.

2

First Interdependency: Consciousness

See how the flowers of the field grow. They do not labor or spin. Yet I tell you that not even Solomon in all his splendor was dressed like one of these.

Matthew 6:28–29, NIV

THE TERM *CONSCIOUSNESS* is not used in a metaphysical way in this book. It simply means to be fully aware without any obstructions. Obstructions to our awareness can take many forms, including lack of mental concentration, oversimplified thinking, false assumptions, unprovable ideas, and indefensible mental models. For individuals and groups, these obstructions create blind spots and make people less conscious. Some might wonder how Christianity and consciousness fit together. However, throughout this book, it should become clearer how the nature of human consciousness influences how Christianity works today, the quality of our Christian lives, and even why Jesus and the Pharisees had so much trouble getting along.

We are all victims of our own unconsciousness. Whether we recognize it or not, we follow outdated rules, oversimplify complex issues, get lost in thought, and fail to fully engage in and appreciate important moments in our lives. We get trapped by what Jesus warned about: our minds labor and spin. When we are unconscious as individuals, we become unable to live like the flowers of the field, unobstructed in the present moment. At the congregational level, when churches are unconscious, people get traumatized.

Conscious individuals and organizations can think more holistically and experience life more fully. But with less consciousness, the Christian faith inevitably becomes more judgmental. In contrast to Jesus' message of love and non-judgment, unconscious Christians easily judge others and themselves, oversimplify ideas as 100% good or bad, learn the wrong lessons from history, and view complicated and controversial actions as either completely right or wrong.[1]

Understanding dualism and non-dualism enters in as well. The nature of dualism is to separate, whereas the nature of non-dualism is to look for connections. There are many examples of dualistic and non-dualistic tensions in the New Testament between Jesus and the Pharisees and Sadducees. The religious leaders of that day loved the law, which was dualistic (i.e., things were either right or wrong), yet Jesus proposed a new model when he said that love fulfilled the law (which was a more non-dualistic approach).[2] Jesus' non-dualism was seen as heretical by the religious elite of the day.

Unconsciously applied dualistic thinking can be seductive because it seems to provide clarity. But with complicated subjects, this oversimplification comes at the expense of greater wisdom and truth. Over time, it increases tribalism and breeds intolerance. In modern life, we see the battle between dualism and non-dualism play out every day. Powerful people (on the right and the left) use dualistic soundbites to keep their flocks separate, afraid, angry, and energized. They

---

[1]Jesus taught, "Do not judge, or you too will be judged. For in the same way you judge others, you will be judged, and with the measure you use, it will be measured to you" (Matt. 7:1–2, NIV).

[2]See Matt. 22:36–40 and Rom. 13:8–10

deliberately oversimplify their positions, emotionalize them, and keep their audiences fired up through steady diets of one-sided arguments and examples.

With greater consciousness, Christians can see context as a friend, which brings with it greater personal and congregational wisdom, curiosity, love, and connection. People with greater consciousness can be more equanimous, are better able to relax in life's uncertainties, resist the temptation of fighting for extreme positions, and experience the "peace that passes understanding" during life's storms.

*   *   *

The nature of consciousness affects the Christian system directly and indirectly in several ways. For example, when people deconstruct, it is often in response to Christian unconsciousness, and their previously held unconscious, judgmental, and unprovable beliefs typically drop away. More conscious qualities like love, compassion, and truth usually remain. "Christianity without dogma," "conscious Christianity," and "Christian consciousness" are used interchangeably in this book because I consider them all to be different ways of saying the same thing.

> *Dualistic thinking has advantages in the physical world, but one of its big disadvantages in social environments is that it increases clarity at the expense of wisdom. In modern life, we are surrounded by misapplied dualism. We only need to see the frequency with which complex issues get distilled into 280-character, one-sided and self-serving tweets. Dualistic people and their organizations create financially successful markets at the extremes. Unfortunately, over time, people who are more balanced eventually lose their voices, tribalism increases, and people get hurt.*

To avoid confusion, however, Christian consciousness is different from what is known as "Christ Consciousness." Christ Consciousness is a metaphysical belief system (and therefore, dogmatic). It is a belief system in search of a higher self as part of a universal system of spiritual awakening. The *Christ* in Christ Consciousness does not refer to Jesus Christ, although proponents often believe Jesus possessed Christ Consciousness.

Another way to think about consciousness is to consider its opposite, unconsciousness. When people are unconscious, they are unaware of their surroundings and unable to respond to their environments. A comatose patient in a hospital is an extreme example of someone who is unconscious. But people do not need to be in a coma to be unconscious. Degrees of unconsciousness can run the gamut, from simply being lost in thought to embracing dangerously unconscious ideologies like racism, misogyny, homophobia, and xenophobia. In the worst cases, it can even result in killing others because they hold different beliefs or are not the "right" kind of people. Could this ever happen to Christianity? Indeed, it has happened many times throughout history.

In Christianity, embracing life as it is with an open mind and loving heart, helping others as Jesus did, and forgiving people like Jesus instead of judging them like the Pharisees are all signs of greater consciousness. As individuals, we become more conscious when we can let go of the mental chatter in our heads, be more open to new ideas, take off our egoic masks, and connect to what we know is true deep in our hearts.

DECONSTRUCTING IN REAL LIFE: *"I spent 20 years as a Christian and had an increasing number of doubts and questions. For many years, I didn't honor my feelings and silenced the inner voice telling me, "This is not right." As I deconstructed, I began to trust that inner voice and through that trust, combined with helpful podcasts and social media, I have been able to become free and think for myself. Now I know I am going to be okay."*

Mindfulness meditation can help to cultivate personal consciousness. During meditation, consciousness is often experienced like a still pond, where we can watch our reflection while understanding that we are not the reflection. We can understand that we are not our thoughts and that bad ideas are only thoughts. Experiencing greater consciousness is like being in an airplane, where we are able to see the blue sky above the gray clouds.

Christians can suspend their judgments and be freer to adapt to new information as consciousness increases. With less consciousness, all they can do is deny the facts and dig in their heels. It's like the story of the ostrich that puts its head in the sand when it sees a lion. Even though it increases its comfort level by blocking out what it does not want to see, its comfort does not last. To be a more conscious Christian is like taking our heads out of the sand and awakening from a dogmatic dream. Being more conscious does not mean we have to have everything figured out. It only requires the wisdom and humility to be able to say three simple words: "I don't know."

DUALITY AND NON-DUALITY

Our consciousness gets cloudier when we see the world in oversimplified, unprovable, and indefensible ways. How we think about dualism and non-dualism significantly affects this. When we think dualistically, we look for differences, like when we see the head and tail as opposite sides of a coin. Non-dualistically, holism is preferred, like when one sees the three dimensions (head, tail, edge) of the coin overall. Through dualism, the mind separates, compares, and contrasts. Through non-dualism, the mind examines the bigger picture and looks for connections and synergies.

In Christianity, fundamentalists tend to be more dualistic about their beliefs, whereas progressives tend to be more non-dualistic. The result is that progressives see fundamentalists as being inflexible, and fundamentalists consider progressives to be wishy-washy. In the Bible, Jesus' message of love fulfilling the law was more non-dualistic. Conversely, the Pharisees' defense of the law was more dualistic.

Both duality and non-duality are important, but when misapplied, duality leads to unconscious thinking and behaviors. Being dualistic is useful when differences matter in the physical world. For example, to be able to distinguish the bed from the bathtub is a conscious, dualistic act. When we drive across a bridge, we can be thankful that the engineers made many dualistic choices consistent with the laws of physics. Non-dualism is a more conscious thinking style that is especially useful when there are many complicated social dynamics to consider.

Despite its tendency to create significant blind spots, dualistic thinking is common and unconscious in complex social environments. Oversimplifying complicated subjects and converting them into crisp soundbites makes them feel clearer (that's the appeal). But by removing the context, what is said is less true (that's the danger).

When Jesus taught that love fulfilled the Jewish law, he was teaching non-dualism over dualism. He was also teaching non-dualism when he said not to look for a speck in the eye of another while ignoring the beam in one's own eye.[3] This was a paradigm shift for the legalistic and dualistic orientations of the religious leaders of the day. To try to help, Jesus used parables. When his disciples asked why, he said, "Though seeing, they do not see; though hearing, they do not hear or understand."[4]

To further illustrate important differences between dualism and non-dualism, the side-by-side comparisons in Table 2.1, "Dualistic Thinking vs. Non-Dualistic Thinking," may help.

This chapter is not an attack on dualism, except for where when misapplied, it makes people less conscious. Large systems, for example, require dualism to scale. The entire computer world would not exist without its binary foundation of ones and zeros. The legal system is also set up dualistically, but with greater imperfections, given the socially complex subject matter: the defense and prosecution are in court to win or lose a verdict and people are found either guilty or not guilty.

Often, when people go through Christian deconstruction, they become less dualistic because of the subject matter. When deconstructing, they are often responding to dualistic religious thinking that has become ideological, with leaders encouraging church members to choose a side and fight for it. Even if these positions don't make sense, they are unable to be changed or even challenged within the church.

[3]See Matt. 7:3–5 and Luke 6:41–42

[4]Matt. 13:13, NIV

Table 2.1. Dualistic Thinking vs. Non-Dualistic Thinking

DUALISTIC THINKING	NON-DUALISTIC THINKING
You or me	You and me
This or that	This and that
Right or wrong	Right and wrong
One thing compared to another	One thing as part of another
Either/or	Both/and
Male or female	Male and female
Explicitly defined	Nuanced
Thinking about the past and future	Directly experiencing this moment
People are threats to each other	People depend upon each other
Bucket of water from a river	Water flowing in a river
Thinking about the parts	Understanding the whole
Religious law	Human love
Egoic thinking	Conscious experience
"I will be" or "I was"	"I am"
Religious concepts	Spiritual connections
Clock time	Timelessness
Left-brained	Right-brained
Striving for what we do not have	Appreciating what we do have
Particle	Wave
Now leads to a destination	*Now* is the destination
Win or lose	Win something while losing something
Inside or outside	Inside and outside
The cost of something	The value of something

DUALISTIC THINKING	NON-DUALISTIC THINKING
Life is form	Life is beyond form
Repeatable	Original
We are in the world	The world is in us
If you want something, take it	If you want something, give it
Human nature is good *or* evil	Human nature is good *and* evil
Words	Ideas
Pieces need to fit together	Pieces do not need to fit together
There is a solution to everything	Some things have no solutions
Ingredients in a cake	Flavor of the cake
Laws of a country	Culture of a country
Striving to eventually achieve a purpose	This moment is the purpose
Nature serves people	People serve nature
Certain	Ambivalent
Finite	Infinite
Living or dying as separate events	Living and dying simultaneously
Controlling	Supporting
Spiritual or religious	Spiritual and religious

Religious dualism is appealing to religious leaders because oversimplified soundbites are easy to create and remember. It is also easier to judge and separate from others than to do the harder work of empathizing and connecting with them. But while dualistic Christians can wag their fingers with righteous indignation at people in another boat, the truth is that they are often on the same river and sometimes even in the same boat. More than 2,000 years after Jesus said it, looking for the speck in another's eye and ignoring the beam in our own continues to haunt us. Harsh judgment of others is misapplied dualism in action. It can lead to considering intolerance as a virtue and believing that for one group to win, another must lose. Unfortunately, when this game plan plays out, over time, *everyone* loses.

If Christians can do a better job of non-dualistically seeing and making more connections between people, groups, issues, stances, and goals, Christianity will inevitably become more conscious. As a result, Christians will become wiser, be able to live better lives, and create better societies. Alternatively, the dualistic walls that Christian leaders build will imprison those on both sides. In the New Testament, the religious leaders were imprisoned by their own dualistic laws. Jesus showed a more conscious alternative by advocating that love could unlock their dogmatic cells.

When Christians are dualistic, they are automatically judgmental, and this stance hurts them as individuals and groups. It's hard for judgmental people to be curious, and because they are not curious, they are not lifelong learners. Their abilities to inquire, investigate multiple perspectives, question the motives of their information sources, and adapt to new and better information over time are limited. Furthermore, their judgmental perspective often results in them exuding confidence without having wisdom, which increases Christian unconsciousness in both word and deed.

THE CONSCIOUS MIND

The quality of our consciousness affects how we see ourselves and the world around us. Our consciousness is not an all-or-nothing proposition. We all regularly experience periods of unconsciousness. The key is to be able to observe these periods as they come and go. Have you ever worried about something that never happened, compulsively agonized over a situation that you wanted to be different than it was, had an imaginary and emotionally heated conversation with someone in your head, or passed an exit while driving as you were lost in thought? All are everyday examples of different states of personal unconsciousness.

One aspect of this, as described earlier, is the unconscious mind's affinity for misplaced dualism: separating, comparing, and embracing thought patterns that are not helpful. It also likes to be in charge, strive for egoic invulnerability, and would rather be wrong than in doubt. It tries to have everything figured out and enjoys the safety of the conceptual world. When times are bad, it laments that others seem to be in better shape than we are. When times are good, it is quick to point out how much better we are than others. The unconscious mind is messed up. If we had friends like this, we would probably ditch them in a heartbeat.

DECONSTRUCTING IN REAL LIFE: *"I was a super-committed Christian, and yet I felt that the church was providing false promises and standards. For example, I was a pastor's kid, and my dad left my mom for a woman at the church. The church protected my father more than my mom because of who he was. I deconstructed because I took my faith seriously and could not take what was going on anymore."*

When we are unconscious as individuals, we miss out on the joy of life itself. Have you ever wasted time worrying about something that never ended up happening rather than engaging directly with a loved one who was sitting right in front of you? Jesus spoke about this when he said, "Look at the birds of the air; they do not sow or reap or store away in barns, and yet your heavenly Father feeds them. Are you not much more valuable than they? Can any one of you by worrying add a single hour to your life?"[5]

Jesus spoke about the unconscious mind in his Sermon on the Mount. In so doing, he followed the prophets and the law in caring about both behaviors and their inner origins. For example, greedy attitudes lead to more greed and selfishness. Jesus used the example of adultery when he said, "You have heard that it was said, 'You shall not commit adultery.' But I tell you that anyone who looks at a woman lustfully has already committed adultery with her in his heart."[6] In saying this, he illustrated how unconscious thoughts often precede

---

[5]Matt. 6:26–27, NIV

[6]Matt. 5:27–28, NIV

unconscious actions. It's like when Paul writes, "I do not understand what I do. For what I want to do I do not do, but what I hate I do."[7] Unconscious thoughts are a source of personal suffering, can often hurt other people, and frequently keep us from living the lives we know we could and should be living.

Unconscious thinking can put us in a perpetual state of misery when we obsessively want things to be different than they are. It is like being on a never-stopping hamster wheel in a self-created cage. When we jump from one goal to another, it is difficult to live consciously in the present moment. Even when people actually achieve the goals they have set, the celebration is short-lived, and the pursuit of the next goal quickly begins, along with the anxiety that comes with it. The world of material success may belong to the go-getters, but it is a largely unconscious world.

One irony associated with unconscious living is that by trying to be happy, we become perpetually unhappy—because we are always striving for the next thing. It turns out that happiness, though, is what is left when we stop looking for it. In any event, even with great success, people's assets often end up owning them before it's over anyway. With greater consciousness, we can enjoy the present moment and truly appreciate the preciousness of life's impermanence. Like the apostle James writes: "Yet you do not know what tomorrow will bring. What is your life? For you are a mist that appears for a little time and then vanishes."[8]

CHRISTIAN CONSCIOUSNESS

So how does all of this consciousness talk apply to Christianity? First, to be more conscious as a Christian means that we need to be more fully aware of and responsive to our direct experience. It means that the path to improving our faith benefits from removing obstructions, welcoming independent opinions, and freeing ourselves from unhealthy dualistic thinking, unproven ideas, and unconscious habits. Like Paul

---

[7] Rom. 7:15, NIV

[8] James 4:14, ESV

wrote in his letter to Roman Christians, we should not conform to this world's pattern but be transformed by the renewing of our minds.

To not be "of the world" does not mean that Christians should separate from their neighbors. Rather, it inspires us to hold what is wrong with the world more loosely and more consciously. By doing this, we can be more conscious as Christians, and Christianity can also become more conscious as a faith. Along this path, deconstructing Christians may find it useful to consider the shifts listed in Table 2.2, "Less Conscious vs. More Conscious Christianity."

Table 2.2. Less Conscious vs. More Conscious Christianity

LESS CONSCIOUS	MORE CONSCIOUS
Focused on ideology	Observational
Lost in thought	Engaged in the moment
Judging	Connecting
Believing the unprovable	Pursuing truth wherever it leads
Ego-based	Selfless
Trapped in discursive thinking	Enjoying mental stillness
Dualistic orientation	Non-dualistic orientation
Tribal	Unified
Intolerant of differences	Curious about differences
Fear-based	Trust-based
Life is black and white	Life is black, white, and gray
Defensive	Vulnerable
Discontented	Content
Attached to concepts	Connected to people
Striving for permanence	Thriving on change

As individuals, Christians can become more conscious by being more fully engaged in the present moment. The present moment is not conceptual. It is the source of our direct experience: it is all that there is, has ever been, or will ever be. We do not live within discrete bands of time. We are part of an unbroken wave that has been in motion for *all* time. Our lives do not start with our births, or our parents, or their parents. We do not live until we die: we are always living and dying at the same time. We are proof of an unbroken flow of life, like the dancer and the dance, the knower and the known, and the air that is not separate from the wind.

Christianity can become more conscious by removing its obstructions, freeing itself from harmful dualistic thinking, letting go of destructive dogma, and just letting love fulfill the law by getting out of Jesus' way. As individual Christians, we can choose to get out of our heads and begin to directly experience an abundant Christian life right here, right now.

Consciousness was the first interdependency that emerged when I deconstructed the Christian system. It paved the way for the next consideration, which was examining the interrelationships between the dualistic nature of religion and non-dualistic spirituality. That is the subject of the next chapter.

CHAPTER SUMMARY IN STORYBOOK FORM

- Once upon a time, Christians were taught that the foundation of their faith was what they believed.
- Every day, they took comfort in the clarity and security that their dogma provided.
- One day, they discovered that their dogmatic and dualistic thinking was making them less conscious. They had become more like the Pharisees and less like Jesus.
- Because of that, they began to lean into Jesus' non-dualistic parables and beatitudes. This helped them become more conscious, which helped them to become more loving.
- Because of that, they became less judgmental and more Christian.
- Until finally, they became more like Jesus: more loving, non-judgmental, forgiving, and helpful to those in need.
- And then they were able to live happily ever after.

3

Second Interdependency: Religion

A horrible and shocking thing has happened in the land. The prophets prophesy falsely, and the priests rule by their own authority. My people love it so, but what will you do in the end?

Jeremiah 5:30–31, ESV

MORE THAN 600 years before the time of Christ, the Judean prophet Jeremiah wrote about what happens when religion loses its spirituality. He saw that prophets lied, priests abused their power, and that people nevertheless seemed happy with it all. Centuries later, Jesus stood up against how religion was being practiced. But, unfortunately, the religious elite chose to cling to their status, control others, impose harsh dogmatic laws, and commercialize their temples. Eventually, religious and political leaders joined forces to kill Jesus after he threatened the Judaic business model by insisting that love should fulfill the law.

Then, like today, there is a constant tension between legalistic religion and the freedom of spirituality. It is like the tension between duality and non-duality. Religion grows through organizational standardization. Spirituality thrives through human connection. Is the best of both worlds even possible? The truth is that each is needed to grow the Christian faith in a healthy way. Religion without spirituality is prone to corruption. Spirituality without religion reduces the faith's capability to make a large social impact.

THE TENSION BETWEEN RELIGION AND SPIRITUALITY

Religion and *spirituality* are often used interchangeably in Christianity, but there are important differences. Religion is designed to scale structurally from the top down (this concept will be further explored in Chapter 5). In contrast, spirituality emerges through individuals, from the bottom up. Religion is designed for groups, whereas spirituality is experienced in a personal way.

> *Jesus showed that like training wheels on a bicycle, religious rules helped people get started and stay within guardrails, but that the rules eventually became hindrances and could be replaced by love. It is a little like the difference between when a parrot talks and when it flies. Religion is like a parrot learning to mimic words. Spirituality is like a parrot spreading its wings and discovering what it was born to be.*

The tension between religion and spirituality played out repeatedly during Jesus' arguments with the Pharisees and Sadducees. In the New Testament, different religious leaders represented different forms of Judaism, somewhat like today's Catholics and Protestants within the Christian faith. Both were legalistic, but a key difference in their case was that the Pharisees believed in an afterlife, whereas the

Sadducees did not. Paul's training as a Pharisee no doubt explains his perspective in his first-century letters to the early Christians.

The Jewish leaders practiced Judaism through their religious laws, but Jesus insisted that love fulfilled those laws. This threatened the value of their religious training and even their livelihoods. While Jesus regularly challenged the religious elite, he did not suggest that spirituality replace religion. The temple was important to him. At the same time, he was visibly angered by the corruption and commercialization of the religion itself. Jesus put a spotlight then on what is a Christian dilemma today: while religion without spirituality is subject to corruption, spirituality without religion is not scalable.

Religion and spirituality have different natures. Spirituality is more like the non-dualism explored in the previous chapter. It exists in the present moment and seeks wisdom and human connection. Religion is more like dualism. Its power comes through doing things as groups that people cannot do as individuals. For example, religious organizations can make significant societal impacts by scaling their organizational capabilities. Modern tensions between religiously dogmatic and spiritually deconstructing Christians are like those that existed between the Jewish leaders and Jesus in the first century. Consider some side-by-side comparisons in Table 3.1, "Religious vs. Spiritual Orientation."

Table 3.1. Religious vs. Spiritual Orientation

RELIGIOUS ORIENTATION	SPIRITUAL ORIENTATION
Dualistic	Non-dualistic
Uses a map	Uses a compass
Strives for certainty	Thrives on ambivalence
Focuses on groups	Individually emerges
Conforms	Explores
Tries to paint the strawberry	Wants to taste the strawberry
Relies on dogmatic beliefs	Relies on direct experience
Reflects light (like the moon)	Produces light (like the sun)
Outside-In	Inside-Out

RELIGIOUS ORIENTATION	SPIRITUAL ORIENTATION
Prescribes answers	Asks questions without needing answers
Like reading sheet music	Like playing jazz
Like painting by numbers	Like painting through inspiration
Like a mounted deer	Like a living deer
About being right	About being true
Formally organized	Personally inspired
Focuses on addition—more is more	Focuses on subtraction—less is more
Closed operating system	Open operating system
Worships via a march	Worships via a dance
Pushed by rules and beliefs	Pulled through purpose and principles
Bounded and unambiguous	Unbounded and ambiguous
Seeks the answer	Attracts the answer
God is an object	God is a mystery
Searches for approval by others	Doesn't require approval from others
We are part of something bigger	Something bigger is part of us
Strives to be powerful	Tries to be vulnerable
Generalizes and imposes itself	Specializes and exposes itself
Does something now for the future	Does something now for this moment
Prays out loud in a talking mode	Meditates in silence in a listening mode
Left-brained and objective	Right-brained and subjective
Separates from others	Connects to others

RELIGIOUS ORIENTATION	SPIRITUAL ORIENTATION
We are our thoughts	We watch our thoughts come and go
Words have authority	Words point to greater meaning
We choose our religious path	Our spiritual path chooses us
About growing up	About waking up
A monologue	A dialogue

In a 2017 survey by the Public Religion Research Institute, 18% of Americans identified themselves as *spiritual but not religious.*[1] They skewed younger and more educated than traditionally religious Americans, with 40% holding at least a four-year college degree and 17% having a postgraduate education. These findings were consistent with the Pew research cited in Chapter 1, which showed that spirituality was increasing even though dogmatic beliefs were losing their relevance.

Being spiritual but not religious is a viable path for many people who deconstruct from the Christian religion. Some get involved in New Age or another brand of mystical spirituality. This often includes a move from dualistic to non-dualistic thinking. When people make this type of switch, new forms of supernatural dogma will often come along for the ride, and along with them come many of the same problems as when Christian churches treat denominational dogma like facts.

When someone deconstructs and becomes spiritual but not religious, being freed from organized religion can feel good. But leaving organized religion behind entirely is not for everyone, and it can be a little like seeing problems with the educational system and deciding to abandon schools altogether. While the future of organized Christianity is unclear (see Chapter 8 for further explanation), in

---

[1] See Daniel Cox & Robert P. Jones, "America's Changing Religious Identity," PRRI (Public Religion Research Institute, June 9, 2017), https://www.prri.org/research/american-religious-landscape-christian-religiously-unaffiliated/.

many cases, improving churches will produce greater benefits than rejecting them entirely.

If churches can be spiritual *and* have strong organizational capabilities, their impact can be multiplied. Christian organizations that are spiritually alive without needing dogmatic thinking can produce many good things. People can form friendships with others who have shared values, participate in meaningful experiences and traditions, help people in need, and collectively achieve higher levels of personal consciousness. In an increasingly ritual-starved society, much good can come from wise Christian traditions that help people achieve positive personal and social outcomes.

DECONSTRUCTING IN REAL LIFE: *"My deconstruction began with questions I ignored for many years. I began deconstructing as a missionary in East Africa. I began seeing the gaps and harm in mission work (aka colonization, power, greed...) and didn't believe it lined up with the person of Jesus. I experienced a lot of Evangelical racism. I'm now reading and finding community. It has cost me a lot. My biggest struggle has been facing, working through, and forgiving myself for all the harm I caused along my devoted path."*

Well-educated and financially secure non-religious pundits will often argue that living fulfilling and moral lives is possible without religion. However, we live in a world where billions of people struggle in serious ways. Many compassionate Christian churches are excellent at helping people inside and outside their sanctuaries. Imagine if more churches could unify their members around Jesus' priorities of love, connection, and service and use their organizational capacities to help people in bigger ways.

Churches, as organizations, can be used for good and evil. This will be covered further in Chapter 5. The deconstruction movement continually shines a light on the fact that there are some bad leaders, harmful churches, and many unconscious practices across the Christian landscape. While abandoning religion may well be the best answer for people who have been traumatized, completely rejecting religion for others would be like rejecting atomic physics because it was used to help design nuclear weapons.

> **DECONSTRUCTING IN REAL LIFE:** *"I am deconstructed but holding onto Jesus (though I am also considered an active deacon in an SBC-affiliated church). I deconstructed for a bunch of reasons. Two of the biggest were (1) acknowledging just how messy the Bible is and that many things I considered black and white are actually quite grey; (2) realizing much of what I had considered to be "Christianity" was actually a cocktail of Western individualism, consumerism, and white supremacy. My biggest current struggle is trying to bear witness to my own journey while not viewing other Christians as incurious simpletons."*

RELIGIOUS CONSCIOUSNESS

When John the Baptist saw the religious leaders coming, he said to them, "You brood of vipers!"[2] He, like Jesus, aimed his spiritual sword at the corruption of the religious system. Jesus said, "Do not suppose that I have come to bring peace to the earth. I did not come to bring peace, but a sword."[3] The Christian deconstruction movement can be this sword.

In the New Testament, without love guiding their religious laws, the temple leaders lost their spiritual compass and became unconscious. Today, many churches have similarly become what the social sciences term "closed systems." Closed systems have weak feedback mechanisms, therefore have little ability to change, and tend to calcify as a result. Dogma increases this calcification in churches because leaders claim it comes from an unchanging, unchangeable, and dogmatic God. In closed systems, religious and otherwise, members typically cling to what has worked in the past. In the New Testament, the religious elite chose the clarity of their dogma over the uncertainty that a love-based religion would have introduced. Jesus made the leaders angry by essentially arguing that religion and spirituality needed to be integrated through love and that love needed to lead the dance.

---

[2]Matt. 3:7, NIV

[3]Matt. 10:34, NIV

The tension between religion and spirituality is ongoing because the nature of each is different. Religion strives for control, whereas spirituality pursues freedom. When organized religion becomes more powerful, its leaders are tempted to strive for greater control, and this ends up killing the spirituality that fueled the faith to begin with. It is like the story of the frog and the scorpion. The scorpion (religion) asks the frog (spirituality) for a ride across the river. The scorpion promises not to kill the frog while it is swimming, as this would not serve either of their interests. But halfway across the river, riding on the back of the frog, the scorpion puts in its stinger.

On their way down, the frog asks, "Why?"

The scorpion confesses, "I could not help it. It is my nature."

Religion requires standardized systems to grow. This requires a checklist of dualistic activities like joining a church, going to church, reading the Bible, believing this but not that, and tithing. On the other hand, spirituality is non-dualistic: it is more about increasing personal consciousness through direct experience in the present moment. Jesus modeled a more spiritual religion, one that focused on loving, accepting, forgiving, and helping others. He tried to spiritually elevate love above the law, and this ultimately led to his crucifixion.

This book highlights the conflicts between the Pharisees and Sadducees and Jesus. Historically and sadly, a focus on those conflicts has allowed Christians to paint the Pharisees and Sadducees as "Jesus killers," which has led to antisemitism over the centuries. However, other than using the exchanges in the New Testament as examples of how dualism is different from non-dualism and religion is different from spirituality, there is no intent here to paint the religious Judaic leaders of the first century in a negative light.

During the first century, the Jewish community in Palestine was under great pressure politically, religiously, culturally, and morally. Already under Greek rule from the 3rd century BC forward, the pressure to assimilate and give up distinctive Jewish ways had been profoundly felt. At this point, Rome was in Palestine, in power. Jewish hopes of self-rule through the restoration of land and king seemed hopelessly frustrated. The community was greatly divided.

During this time, the Pharisees tried a path of religious separatism by steering clear of the Romans and intensifying Jewish rituals and legal observances to please God and stay pure. The Jewish political authorities were trying to appease Rome and keep the lid from blowing off. Jesus, a deeply Jewish figure, came bringing a very different vision and practice during a very tense time. These conflicts are forcefully highlighted in the New Testament gospels.

*   *   *

By openly questioning the faith, Christian deconstruction has the potential to help Christians and some churches reconnect spirituality and religion. This brings with it the potential to help people live better and more Jesus-centric lives in a more systematic way. The religious Christian ecosystem is a group of assets that can either continue to decline or be reinvented by transcending outdated dogmatic beliefs and practices. Christianity can be looked at in two ways: as an unrealized asset or a burning platform.

Christianity as a religion can help people accomplish together what they cannot achieve as individuals. Though Jesus battled with the religious leaders of the day and was eventually killed because of it, he never suggested that people give up on religion. He simply encouraged religious leaders to transcend their rigid, religious rules. Jesus showed that like training wheels on a bicycle, religious rules helped people get started and stay within guardrails, but that the rules eventually became hindrances and could be replaced by love. It is a little like the difference between when a parrot talks and when it flies. Religion is like a parrot learning to mimic words. Spirituality is like a parrot spreading its wings and discovering what it was born to be.

Religion provides a container that can be filled by non-dogmatic spirituality. Religion without non-dogmatic spirituality is easy to spot. There is little love and a large misuse of supernatural power. Spirituality without religion is also easy to spot. People feel good, but there is little social impact. Without enough religious structure, people can read spiritual books, watch inspiring videos, and listen to wonderful music, but not make a meaningful difference for people who desperately need help. On the other hand, without a meaningful spiritual practice, it is hard to tell the difference between Christians in church and the Pharisees in the New Testament.

Jesus asked Judaic religious leaders to be more spiritual through being more loving. Today, despite Christianity's declines in church attendance and relevance, and an ever-increasing Evangelical militancy, the Christian religion's infrastructure is a global treasure that possesses within it a nearly unparalleled ability to make a difference in people's lives in struggling communities around the world.

Christians can be more conscious, spiritual, and religiously impactful. One thing that almost always gets in the way, and that deconstructing Christians often begin with, is unchallengeable church dogma, which is the third interdependency in the Christian system and the subject of the next chapter.

CHAPTER SUMMARY IN STORYBOOK FORM

- Once upon a time, Christians were very religious.
- Every day, they focused on their church rituals and clung to their religious beliefs and practices.
- One day, they discovered that they were acting more like the Pharisees than like Jesus.
- Because of that, they became more spiritual as they practiced their Christian faith. This made them more joyful.
- Because of that, they reconnected their religion and spirituality, and each was able to strengthen the other.
- Until finally, they became more like Jesus. More loving, less judgmental, more forgiving, and better at helping people in need.
- And then they were able to live happily ever after.

4

Third Interdependency: Dogma

The entire law is fulfilled in keeping this one command:
"Love your neighbor as yourself."

Galatians 5:14, NIV

DOGMA IS A popular springboard for deconstructing Christians. It usually starts when someone questions a specific dogmatic belief that doesn't seem to add up, often related to something like the nature of God, what God is said to care about culturally, the authority of the Bible, or the origin of the universe. These discussions usually hit roadblocks because dogma is largely unchangeable and unchallengeable, hidden within religious black boxes, and defended by church authorities who are paid to protect it. Adding to the difficulty, hell sometimes lingers in the background, raising the stakes for being wrong. The result? The truth that can set people free is limited to what their churches have already told them to believe. This then leads them elsewhere.

Dogma can be influenced in many ways, including by national culture, church history, political leanings, and family traditions.

Dogmatic debates don't usually help much because they are designed to reinforce the party line, no matter what. Church leaders do not have the authority to do anything other than defend church doctrine, and professional apologists, to quote Jesus, seem to be well trained to strain out the gnats yet swallow the camel.[1]

Christians are taught that dogma is the truth that led to the formation of the church, but it is much more probable that things happened the other way around. Church business models were built around their dogma, made sure it couldn't be challenged, trained people to defend it, manufactured spiritual problems and proprietary solutions, and established penalties for not believing. Then churches charged their members money for all of this.

Dogma is a byproduct of business models. If a denomination's theological model is constructed around original sin, it's easy to find Bible verses that emphasize an angry God, harsh judgment, and eternities in hell for nonbelievers. Yet if the business model were to be constructed around Jesus' love and forgiveness, different Bible verses—those on mercy, grace, and service—could just as easily be emphasized. The Bible verses that churches use are a little like the notes in a musical score. The same notes can play different songs, and the same Bible can support different Christian narratives.

*　*　*

The Bible is a collection of books filled with insights and inspiration, as well as snapshots of ancient barbarisms. It is the church's book and the Jewish people's book, a treasured heirloom that doesn't require being considered factually perfect. The idea of inerrancy, which will be covered later in this chapter, doesn't fit with the nature of the Bible itself. The Bible is filled with poetry, fables, songs, and genres never intended to make sense when read literally. The Bible is a treasure, but it is not factual, provable, or true or false in the same way empirical and historical claims are.

The goal of this chapter is not to undermine beliefs that are meaningful to readers. If someone has dogmatic beliefs, that if they were

---

[1]Matt. 23:34

to abandon them, would make them fundamentally different than who they are and who they wish to be, then certain of these may be good dogmatic beliefs. Our beliefs are often not provable like math equations, yet we all live our lives by them, and they are valuable when they make our lives better. (The problem with dogma that I focus on in this chapter occurs when unprovable beliefs are imposed on others.) If people were free to abandon them, it would in turn help them live better, more authentic, and more Jesus-centric lives.

Christian dogma is like a tangled ball of yarn. It is possible to believe in Jesus' message of love as his commandment yet be infuriated by the Christian church and many of the faith's obvious charlatan leaders. It is also possible to see flaws in various religious practices yet cherish the positive role that the Christian faith can play in people's lives. Through a message of loving God and others, inspirational music, holiday traditions, transcendent experiences, and meaningful personal relationships that can be found in community, church has potential for good.

With all these complexities in mind, the path for deconstructing Christians is not a one-size-fits-all solution because different people have very different Christian experiences and personal backgrounds. In this chapter, as a reminder, dogma is defined as having three characteristics:

1. Claimed to be true by someone in authority;
2. cannot be proven by outsiders; and
3. is unable to be honestly challenged by insiders.

INSIDE THE DOGMATIC HORNET'S NEST

Dogma is an important part of the Christian system, and it does not supernaturally come out of thin air. It is influenced by history, cultural beliefs, and religious business models, and it benefits from being understood in this way during the deconstruction process. Looking at Christianity as a system is helpful: it's like how once we know that the earth is a sphere versus being flat, and that the earth revolves around the sun versus the other way around, we can more productively talk about sunrises and sunsets. Thinking about dogma in a systematic way can help Christians deconstruct with greater clarity and less trauma.

Just because dogma is not provable does not mean that it is stupid. No one can factually prove everything they believe. Our beliefs are complicated and influenced by many known and unknown interactions within our minds, cultures, histories, physiologies, and who knows how many other things. There is, however, a continuum of defensibility for what we believe. In ancient times, dogma no doubt helped to unify tribes, but the ongoing declines in Christian affiliation over the decades seem to show that it is now having the opposite effect.

The Catholic faith is centrally organized, and therefore its dogma is fairly standard. Among more decentralized Protestant denominations, there is more variety. In the Christian ecosystem, there are theological debates around dogma between Catholics and Protestants, liberals and conservatives, and theists and atheists that seem to go on in perpetuity. The leaders of each side are paid to reinforce their dogmatic brands. They know they are not to deviate from the party line, as doing so would undermine the interests of their employers and put the loyalty of their followers at risk.

To disentangle the ball of yarn, it is useful to consider differences between knowledge, beliefs, and truth. In this book, *knowledge* is something that can be proven by outsiders, such as 2 + 2 = 4. *Beliefs* can be backed up by knowledge, but sometimes they are not. *Truth* is where knowledge and beliefs intersect. Truth is a knowledge-based belief, provable by independent outsiders. Dogma, because it is not provable by independent outsiders, does not qualify as verifiable truth. This does not make dogma automatically false, but it does mean that it is not provable.

With the following illustration, I will begin by emphasizing two rules from the famous statistician George Box for models. All are wrong, but some are useful. In this spirit, figure 4.1 illustrates religious truth as an intersection between factual knowledge and dogmatic beliefs.

Figure 4.1. Knowledge, Truth, and Dogmatic Beliefs

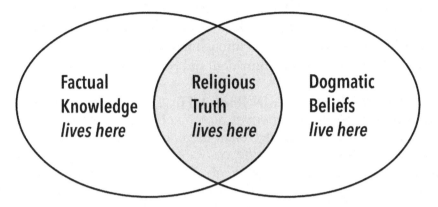

Beliefs that are not verifiably true are not necessarily bad. Two parents can believe their baby is the cutest in the world yet also be pretty sure that their belief is not factually true. The problem is not that there are unverifiable beliefs in Christianity. The problem is mistaking them for religious truth, especially when they are harmful to others, and demanding that others accept them as true.

Jesus shed light on this problem during his battles with the Pharisees. Religious leaders in ancient times, like today, attributed their dogmatic beliefs to God. They did this to try to claim that their beliefs were true. But, like dried cement, once the dogma had been set, it became nearly impossible to change. This led to the great biblical irony of the religious leaders plotting to kill the son of the very God they claimed to serve.

Dogma is often used as a means of control. In the Bible, like today, it was used to control members through a well-developed system of religious education, temples, rituals, laws, and holidays. In addition, religious beliefs have been imposed by force through practices running the gamut from ostracism to stoning people to death. Dogma is an important part of the Christian control system, is reinforced through peer pressure and family expectations, and is often embedded in national politics.

When Christian dogma was developed, it borrowed heavily from the Jewish dogma that was already in place. This is not surprising given that Jesus and his disciples were Jewish and that the Apostle Paul was a trained Pharisee. For more than 1,500 years after the time of Christ, the Christian business model was built around the dogma of original sin, which was perpetuated by and through the Catholic church, continued through the Protestant Reformation, and is still with us today.

> **DECONSTRUCTING IN REAL LIFE:** *"I began deconstructing because my lived experiences directly conflicted and cast much doubt on the things my religious leaders had taught me for 25 years. I began to see the cracks and holes and canyons of disconnect in their teachings. My biggest struggle for sure has been patriarchy and the immoral way many men (and women) have upheld systems that directly harm women."*

Judaism was based on a story about God's covenant history with Israel. As a Jew, Jesus inherited that story and offered his own rendering of it. So did all early Christian leaders, all of them Jews first. Dogma can be understood as an effort to abstract from its narrative specific beliefs the community has come to cherish.

But as organizational power and Christian dogma became inextricably intertwined, many churches used their authority to punish those who challenged them, including burning people at the stake until the early 1800s. While Christian churches have not legally been in the business of killing heretics for two centuries, dogma-related emotional trauma continues to this day and is a common catalyst for why people choose to deconstruct.

So how does dogma come into existence? Largely, it is through organizations and committees. We don't have to go back thousands of years to find an example. Even though it was said not to have "credal weight," the dogma of biblical inerrancy—belief that the Bible was essentially supernaturally and timelessly created—has super-credal weight in the business models of many of today's Evangelical churches. But the reclamation and super-charging of biblical inerrancy did not come down from heaven. Over a short three-day period in October of 1978, more than 200 white, male Evangelical leaders—most, if not all, of whom already earned their livings promoting adherence to inerrancy—wrote the Chicago Statement on Biblical Inerrancy.

The Chicago Statement was created by men who said they believed they knew what God wanted. While the concept of inerrancy certainly existed before, since the statement's publication, biblical inerrancy has been used more forcefully by fundamentalists to condemn those who do not believe that this model of Christianity is God's one true way. The Chicago statement, stored in the Dallas Theological Seminary Archives, significantly influences Evangelical theology and politics to this day. It says that the Bible must be acknowledged as the Word of God by virtue of its divine origin. "Divine origin" is a belief that does not meet the standard for truth described earlier. Rather, it is what this group of Evangelical men pronounced truth to be because it served their purposes. It requires theologians, ministers, and members to believe that the Bible was essentially written, assembled, edited, and translated without error via the Holy Spirit and God's supernatural, invisible hand over thousands of years. It requires believing that the Bible is a literal account of everything from the creation of the universe, to the importance of Bronze Age-morality applied forevermore, to how the world is supposed to end.

Of course, the end of the world in the sense that Jesus talked about it was supposed to have happened 2,000 years ago (yet with many fundamentalist leaders, "hope" seems to spring eternal). Jesus said that the end times would be fulfilled in the generation of that day (Matt. 24:34, Mark 13:30), that some who were standing there would not taste death before they saw the kingdom of God (Luke 9:27), and that the current generation would not pass away until all these things had happened (Luke 21:32).

In addition to the Christian church's systematic use of dogma, friends and family also play a powerful role in using dogmatic beliefs to keep people in the fold. It can be very traumatic for Christians to break away from dogma-influenced relationships, especially when the idea of eternal punishment is part of the equation. Out of respect for parents, spouses, children, and friends, the pressure to go along with toxic beliefs can be intense. Of course, it is not always easy to tell just how strongly Christians believe what they say they believe. For example, Christians who say they look forward to going to heaven usually don't seem particularly anxious to get there when they receive a bad medical diagnosis.

DOGMA'S BIG PROBLEM

Imagine being on vacation in a strange town with a group of friends when your partner suddenly becomes terribly ill. You rush him to the nearest hospital. There, you see a large banner proclaiming Hippocrates as the future of medicine. You are told that in this hospital, the doctors are believers in old-time medicine and that they are the *one true way* physicians. Under the banner "Make Medicine Great Again," the staff proudly explain how they use the best leeches for bloodletting, are experts at drilling holes in people's heads to treat migraines, are at the leading edge of medical flagellation, believe that hand washing is a conspiracy theory, and have plenty of mercury on hand to treat whatever ails you.

DECONSTRUCTING IN REAL LIFE: *"I am a gay 30-year-old male. I increasingly deconstructed as I could no longer tolerate the hypocrisy, hate, racism, manipulation, or people hijacking the Bible to support white supremacy. As a healthcare worker who was watching many people dying, I couldn't stand any longer how Evangelicals were spreading lies about masks and how radicalized Christians were doing anything possible to maintain control."*

Beliefs that are not free to evolve do not lead people to good places.

In the same way that history is written by conquerors, dogma is written by the leaders of organizations who have built business models around it. Using the same Bible, Christian dogma has been used to uplift and instruct, or to condemn and control. To uplift others, the Bible can be used to show how Jesus asked those who had not sinned to cast the first stone, fed the hungry, and helped the sick. On the other hand, with fear and control as the intent, the same Bible can be used to encourage followers to fight unjustified wars, and oppress women, black and indigenous people, people of color, and non-heterosexuals. Either way, biblical dogma can be used in the name of God.

A big problem with dogma, like in the "Make Medicine Great Again" analogy, is its inability to be modified or challenged. When Christians have unalterable answers and require that these answers be unchallenged, congregations can no longer learn through honest inquiry. The truth cannot set them free. Consider the conflicts between religion and science. The conflict between enforcing dogma and pursuing truth is not new. Galileo was proclaimed a heretic by the Catholic Church in 1616 for claiming that the earth was not the center of the universe and in 1633 for proposing that the earth revolved around the sun. He spent the end of his life under house arrest because of it. It took the Catholic Church 359 years to officially admit that Galileo was correct.

How Christians use dogma is a choice. It can be used as a non-negotiable directive said to come from God Almighty, or it can be used to help point people to greater spiritual truths, as was the case when Jesus used parables. Throughout the Bible, and ever since its books were written, religiously powerful people have weaponized dogma by claiming it to be the *literal* truth. But in the New Testament, Jesus continually reframed dogma as *pointing* to the truth. Some examples are in Table 4.1, "Jesus Reframes Dogma."

Table 4.1. Jesus Reframes Dogma

RELIGIOUS LEADERS FRAMING DOGMA	JESUS REFRAMING DOGMA	BIBLICAL REFERENCES
They sought a sign from heaven	There was to be no sign	Mark 8:11–12
Argued about dogma	Jesus reframed dogma	Matthew 19:3–9 Mark 7:5–7 Mark 10: 2–9
Asked a political question	Jesus separated religion from politics	Matthew 22:15–22 Mark 12:28–34 Luke 20:21–25
Condemned a sinner based on the law	Jesus asked those without sin to cast the first stone	John 8:3–11

RELIGIOUS LEADERS FRAMING DOGMA	JESUS REFRAMING DOGMA	BIBLICAL REFERENCES
Asked for the greatest commandment in the law	Jesus said it was loving God and others, which was not even one of their laws	Matthew 22:34–36
The temple was like a marketplace with money changers	Jesus angrily called the temple a den of thieves	Luke 19:45–46
Spewed condemnation for breaking a religious rule	Jesus said that helping others was more important	Matthew 12:1–13 Mark 3:1–6 Luke 6: 6-11
Condemned someone for breaking a religious rule	Jesus reframed the rule	Matthew 12:1–8 Mark 2:23–24 Luke 6:1–5
Loved their power	Jesus condemned their love of power	Mark 12:38–40 Luke 20:45–47
Were concerned with outer appearance	Jesus said they should be concerned with the inside and helping the poor	Luke 11:39–40
Questioned Jesus on the law	Jesus said their training kept them and others from knowing the truth	Luke 11:52–53
Condemned Jesus for associating with sinners	Jesus responded they were who he should be with; the righteous were beyond hope	Matthew 15:1–7 Mark 2:17 Luke 15:2

APOLOGETICS AND DOGMA

Apologetics is a religious discipline responsible for defending dogma through systematic argumentation and discourse. It is part of the Christian system, a defense mechanism against people who are deconstructing, and a systematic way for denominations to internally defend their dogmatic belief systems.

Normally, it would be odd to work in an organization with a department responsible for convincing employees to believe things that independent people thought were false. To what degree does the very existence of apologists signal a truth problem? Do schools need their arithmetic teachers to fly around the world and hold conferences to defend that 2 + 2 = 4? The field of apologetics is required because denominational dogma cannot stand on its own. It is like the religious equivalent of tobacco companies hiring scientists to conduct studies to prove that smoking is not harmful.

Apologetics and unprovable dogma go together like peas and carrots. Apologists are paid to convincingly articulate that their denominational positions are correct and that people outside their group are incorrect. In business language, they are paid to keep consumers believing and buying.

DECONSTRUCTING IN REAL LIFE: *"I deconstructed because the church was incapable of loving people for who they were. There was little to no social conscience for justice, the homeless, or suffering. People were mistreated and suppressed, and the Bible was misused for political purposes. I found that non-church people were helping others more than church people, so I decided to join them."*

In Christianity, the Apostle Paul set the stage by defending his core Pharisaic beliefs while making a minimal number of Gentile-focused concessions on things like circumcision and dietary laws so that he could unify and expand the movement. Paul extended the original sin theology he believed as a Pharisee, which was later institutionalized by the Catholic Church and carried forward by Protestant reformers. Had Paul been a Sadducee instead of a Pharisee, Christianity would likely be different today. For example, the idea of an afterlife might never have been incorporated into its beliefs.

Over the centuries, Christian apologists have influenced the faith. Some popular Evangelical apologists during my lifetime included men like C.S. Lewis with *Mere Christianity* in the 1950s, Francis Schaeffer in the 1970s with his book and video series *How Should We Then Live*, and Josh McDowell, also popular in the 1970s and beyond. Josh McDowell's son Sean built upon his father's book, *Evidence that Demands a Verdict*, in 2017. Of course, there are many others, including Ravi Zacharias mentioned earlier, and many non-Evangelical apologists, but their roles are similar: to defend the faith as being true and to keep believers believing in their denominational dogma.

DECONSTRUCTING IN REAL LIFE: *"I was raised non-denominational and home-schooled, so I was saturated with creationism, purity culture, and apologetics. I tried to be a super-Christian all my life. When I began to deconstruct, my parents turned against me and said I was never a Christian. I have gone from a Jesus-follower, to a progressive, to a hopeful agnostic, and I am now a journeying atheist."*

While dogmatic specifics vary across Christian groups, there are similarities in how apologists practice their trade. When apologists build their cases, they typically begin by saying they were at one point nonbelievers and were convinced to change their minds due to compelling information. For the apostle Paul, his conversion on the road to Damascus changed him from Christian-hater Saul to Christianity-creator Paul. C.S. Lewis and Josh McDowell claimed to first be nonbelievers (an atheist and an agnostic, respectively) before becoming Christians. Schaeffer claimed to grow up non-religious, and Sean McDowell took up his dad's mantle after claiming he had doubts before embracing his father's faith.

A common practice of apologists is to take a provable fact, mix it with an opinion, and convincingly declare that the combination remains factual. To be fair, apologists are not the only dogmatists (religious, political, or otherwise) to do this. Lewis wrote *Mere Christianity* as an intellectual outsider, Schaeffer positioned himself like an erudite scholar, and both McDowells used data-heavy approaches. But despite their differences, each mixed facts with dogma-based opinions as they tried to keep their audiences in the fold. While it's possible that apologists believe what they are saying, the apologetic practice is deceitful in the sense that deceit is neither true nor false but an obscure combination of both. Ironically, Satan was called the great deceiver for similar reasons.

The target audiences for apologists are believers who need a periodic dogmatic pep talk to keep them committed and in the fold. Apologists are good communicators, tend to talk fast, speak with authority, and provide more details in unfamiliar combinations than the average person can intellectually absorb and challenge. Their specious messages are compelling enough to keep those Christians who already believe to continue believing.

SYNTHESIZING SOME EVANGELICAL APOLOGETIC CLASSICS

As a young Christian, I was raised on the three apologetics books mentioned in the previous section, and I read them with no questions asked. Given my age and my environment, they made perfect sense to me. When writing *this* book, I re-read them again. I couldn't help but read them differently as someone in my 60s versus how I read them as a teenager. This section summarizes my "second look" at all three.

In *Mere Christianity*, C.S. Lewis writes that the truth is more important than what pleases someone, that people have an inner compass, and that no one perfectly lives up to their own standards.[2] He crosses the line into dogma when he claims that this inner compass is proof of "the creator God." He takes liberties by speaking on God's behalf, thereby positioning his opinions as unassailable. He describes God as separate and terrifying, then crosses the line again by claiming that the views he holds are evidence that Christianity is the one right answer and that only Christians can live transformed lives. Throughout the

---

[2]C.S. Lewis, *Mere Christianity*. New York: MacMillan Publishers, 1952.

book, Lewis raises rhetorical arguments and then confidently answers them, thereby winning the debates he has with himself.

Lewis defines theology as the "science of God." While at the beginning of his book he claims *not* to speak for Christianity, he ends up doing so throughout the book. *Mere Christianity* was a product of its time, and many 21st-century readers will find it both misogynistic and homophobic.

While Lewis wrote specifically for readers in 1950s Great Britain, Schaeffer and the McDowells wrote for American Evangelicals, largely beginning in the 1970s. A notable difference between them is that Lewis embraces the theory of evolution while Schaeffer and the McDowells steer away from this subject, likely due to the unsupportive feelings of American Evangelicals toward Darwinism.

Schaeffer's *How Should We Then Live* beat the drum for a fundamentalist Christian worldview with a European flair.[3] In his book and videos, Schaeffer played the part of a Swiss intellectual (even though he was originally from Philadelphia), dressing in a traditional Alpine style. He drew conservative conclusions using a relatively complex storyline, incorporating a mixture of history, art, music, literature, politics, philosophy, and architecture. He was like other Evangelical apologists in that he mixed facts and personal opinions and declared the combination to be factual.

Josh McDowell was arguably the best-known and most successful Evangelical apologist of the 20th century, and Sean McDowell has effectively followed in his father's footsteps more recently. The revised 2017 version of Josh and Sean McDowell's *Evidence that Demands a Verdict* builds upon the 1972 version and is nearly 800 pages long.[4] It makes the case that because the Bible has been carefully maintained and has shown excellent consistency over the years, that proves it came from God. Since it came from God, it is therefore inerrant. Their conclusions are consistent with the claims made in The Chicago Statement on Biblical Inerrancy. Josh McDowell, incidentally, was one of the Evangelical leaders who developed that statement, as was Frances Schaeffer.

[3]Francis A. Schaeffer, *How Should We Then Live? The Rise and Decline of Western Thought and Culture.* Grand Rapids, MI: F. H. Revell Company, 1976.

[4]Josh McDowell & Sean McDowell, *Evidence that Demands a Verdict: Life-Changing Truth for a Skeptical World.* Nashville, TN: Thomas Nelson, 2017.

* * *

Believing unchallengeable dogma limits people's abilities to think independently and grow through greater experience and knowledge. Once they agree not to think for themselves, things that would ordinarily not be believable can more easily become so, especially when preached with repetition by their respected authority figures. When audience members give up their right to think independently, leaders are only constrained by their consciences when it is in their personal interests to manipulate their followers with lies.

> **DECONSTRUCTING IN REAL LIFE:** *"My deconstruction started because of gender roles. I couldn't lead men at my church, yet I was leading men in my campus ministry. I was a leader, more specifically a pastor—without the label. My discrimination led me to look at other discrimination. I couldn't and didn't stop at gender roles. My biggest struggle was reconciling my reading of the Bible with what I knew to be abuse and harm in the church. I am still rebuilding the lens through which I read the Bible."*

The practice of combining facts with opinions and claiming the combinations to be factual spreads from leaders to followers very easily. For example, when researching this book, I watched an interview with a Christian woman who answered an interviewer's question about why God allowed suffering. In her response, she mixed what she did know with what she did not know, using the combination of the two to validate her already held dogmatic belief system. She said, "Well, we don't know the mind of God, but we know God has a purpose for everything, and it is because of Adam's original sin that bad things happen today." In dissecting this short sentence, after first claiming that she did not know the mind of God, she immediately crossed the line and said she knew God had a purpose for everything. She connected what she claimed she did not know, to what she claimed to know, to what she could not possibly know, and used it all to repeat with confidence the dogma she had been taught.

Dogma is complicated.

Within the Christian system, there are often unstated assumptions guiding various dogmatic beliefs, which is one reason why the same Bible can mean so many things to different Christians and Christian groups. People argue perpetually about the meaning of individual Bible verses because they have different lenses for their interpretations. This has always been the case. For the Pharisees in the New Testament, the conceptual model seemed to be the law. For Jesus, it seemed to be love. They used the same scriptures but argued due to different interpretations.

Dogma is not categorically stupid. No one can factually prove everything they believe. Our beliefs are complicated and influenced by many known and unknown interactions within our minds, cultures, histories, physiologies, and who knows how many other things. There is, however, a continuum of defensibility for what we believe. In ancient times, dogma no doubt helped to unify tribes, but the ongoing declines in Christian affiliation over the decades seem to show that it is now having the opposite effect.

One of the underlying assumptions guiding a lot of Christian dogma is the nature of the Bible. Every denomination has a point of view. Within evangelicalism, the idea of biblical inerrancy certainly did not begin in 1978, but it *was* elevated and to some degree militarized through the Chicago Statement on Biblical Inerrancy.

Biblical inerrancy is in many ways the foundation of the Evangelical business model. The canonization process was completed by the 4th century, Luther cut some books out during the Reformation, created a German version in 1534, and then the King James version was completed in 1611. So, the "inerrant" version of the Bible that we have today did not exist for more than 1,500 years after the time of Christ. The Evangelical foundation of biblical inerrancy incorporates the mantra of "Every word inspired; every word preached." But this mantra is not actually true because every word is not preached—only the ones that fit the underlying fundamentalist narrative. That narrative is one that has been created and sustained by straight white conservative males.

While fundamentalists insist that the Bible is God's absolute truth, their personal, cultural, political, and denominational beliefs strongly influence which verses they emphasize. Even within evangelicalism, the same Bible is interpreted *very* differently when it comes to matters like speaking in tongues. Like the Pharisees in Jesus' time, dogmatic Christian leaders may speak with pious confidence but ultimately stand upon the fragile dogmatic foundations that they themselves have constructed.

ATHEISM AND DOGMA

Dogma exists in many forms. For example, consider debates between Christians and atheists. Like all debates, they involve people who have something to prove on opposing sides. While celebrity atheists such as Richard Dawkins are only one faction within atheism, I will focus on high-profile atheists in the same way that I have tended to focus on higher-profile parts of the Christian system.

Celebrity atheists and celebrity Christian fundamentalists have similar blind spots. One group tries to disprove the existence of a God that cannot be disproven, while the other group tries to prove the existence of a God they cannot prove. The interactions can be fascinating. Without either side first agreeing on definitions or their underlying assumptions, both sides attack the weaknesses of the other's arguments. Like modern-day gladiators in conceptual colosseums, each debater's audience thirsts for pithy put-downs of the other side.

DECONSTRUCTING IN REAL LIFE: *"For me, the turning point toward deconstruction happened when I began studying intersex people and just how much the male-female theology, and black and white theology more generally, broke down. The church teachings just didn't match reality. It was misinformed and cruel about things like LGBTQ, misogyny, racism, and colonialism."*

The problem is not that dogmatic Christians are wrong and celebrity atheists have it all figured out, or vice versa. Both sides discard honest conversation to win arguments and are often more interested in making a point than in making a difference. With this mindset, empathy and honesty have been largely dispensed with. What results are middle-school insults from people trying to be clever instead of wise and moats being built instead of bridges. Atheist debaters seem to love to target right-wing Christians, make them look foolish, and then generalize their atheistic arguments to Christianity overall. They frame up flaws based on scientific evidence, and then, declaring the other person wrong, pronounce themselves right. In this sense, celebrity atheists are like celebrity apologists.

Atheists can be every bit as dogmatic as fundamentalist Christians, ignoring that Christianity as a system is more than its dogma. Despite the intellectual arrogance of certain celebrity atheists, atheistic organizations are categorically unimpressive by Christian standards. Atheistic groups tend to be led by relatively small numbers of white men talking largely to themselves, full of themselves, and tone-deaf to their extraordinarily hurtful and hateful rhetoric. Despite snubbing religion, atheists themselves are often guilty of worshipping at the altar of natural selection, which tends to be their go-to explanation for things they cannot prove.

Atheistic dogmatists tend to work at the relatively easy level of thought experiments as contrasted to the messy world of real life. Living in the realm of abstract thinking minimizes the many challenges associated with putting one's hypotheses into practice. When a celebrity atheist wants to make a clever put-down, it takes a few seconds. When the Pope wants to change something, even if it is small, he needs to make the change through 1.3 billion people around the world in a way that is compatible with over 2,000 years of history, rituals, and precedents. The degrees of difficulty are not comparable in the slightest.

Since atheism, like Christian dogmatism, operates at a conceptual level, dogmatic atheists have a largely unstated "If you don't like religion, you're going to hate what replaces it" problem. However, despite religion's problems, it is unclear what will happen in society if certain Christian traditions and beliefs deteriorate. Could some end up being like unseen social support beams? Just like physical support beams for homes, if problems with the beams are ignored during a remodel, the houses will become less stable, even to the point of collapse.

Nonetheless, atheists have valid points for Christians to consider. Isn't it unwise for Christians to unconsciously cling to 1st-century dogmatic beliefs in the 21st century? If the Christian faith can't relate to dogma differently, at what point will the continuous membership declines bring Christian fixed-cost overheads crashing down upon even larger numbers of churches? Also, as moderates leave, how much more radical will those who remain become?

Challenging Christian dogma is not easy. A good example of how difficult it is to tamper with it occurred in 2016 when Andy Stanley, founder of North Point Ministries, produced a series of sermons entitled *Who Needs God*. In the series, he talked about the celebrity atheists referred to as "the four horsemen"—Sam Harris, the late Christopher Hitchens, Richard Dawkins, and Dan Dennison. Stanley was one of very few people in the world who had the Evangelical standing to even bring up the subject of challenging certain dogmatic boundaries, which he did in this series. But, despite his power and popularity—including a multi-campus megachurch with 40,000 people attending per Sunday—Stanley was quickly and concertedly condemned by Christian fundamentalists for playing fast and loose with the Bible. In his *Aftermath* series in 2018, Stanley further infuriated fellow fundamentalists when he said that scripture alone was not the authority. If the foundation of the faith was a book, he said, "Good luck with that. The gig is up."

In the Bible, Jesus says that he did not come for the righteous.[5] Perhaps this was not because Jesus thought the righteous had it all figured out, but because he knew they were beyond hope, trapped within the prisons of their dogmatic beliefs, teachings, and systems.

ADAM-BASED AND JESUS-CENTRIC CHRISTIAN MODELS

While Christians don't think of their faith as Adam-based, I will lay out an Adam-based versus Jesus-centric Christian model in this section, suggesting that the predominant Christian theological model is Adam-based and that this is increasingly problematic. Adam is barely mentioned outside of Genesis 1–5, and Paul discusses Adam only three

---

[5]Luke 5

times. Yet the linkage is that through the story of Adam, Judaism established original sin, original sin resulted in blood sacrifices, and Jesus dying for the sins of the world was the ultimate blood sacrifice. But this model is a choice. The model could just as easily be based upon what Jesus said was most important. Could a theological model based on Jesus' priorities in the New Testament instead of on Adam eating a piece of forbidden fruit in Genesis be one worth considering?

In a strange way, many of today's science versus Christianity debates are rooted in the Adam-based dogmatic model. Beginning with evolution versus creation arguments, the often-unspoken issue for fundamentalists is not that some people believe that the universe was created in one week or that humanity began with two fully evolved people. Instead, the problem is that without Adam and Eve and the Garden of Eden, the original sin-based Christian business model is significantly weakened.

Throughout history, part of the Christian business model has depended on its members literally believing that God was so enraged when Adam ate a piece of fruit in the Garden of Eden that he eventually had to kill his only son so that people who became Christians could avoid hell after they died. This narrative has funded the Christian system from its beginning. Yet, ironically, Adam's original sin, which is said to have angered God so much for so long, was his attempt to be able to discern right from wrong, which was also the goal of the Old Testament laws—the same laws that Jesus said should be replaced by love in the New Testament.

Dogma can be puzzling.

Heaven and hell are important ingredients in the Adam-based original sin business model for fundamentalists. Yet, when the afterlife-believing Pharisees and afterlife-denying Sadducees asked Jesus technicalities about who would be part of the resurrection and in what manner, Jesus said that God was not the God of the dead, but of the living.[6] His statement was consistent with an Old Testament verse found in Ecclesiastes on this subject: "The fates of both men and beasts are the same: As one dies, so dies the other—they all have the same breath. Man has no advantage over the animals."[7] As a trained Pharisee, Paul incorporated his beliefs in an afterlife when he wrote his letters to early Christians.

---

[6]Mark 12:27

[7]Ecc. 3:19, BSB

ONE BIBLE, TWO BIBLICAL MODELS

I love the Bible. But the same Bible can be explained in different ways using different underlying theological models. One is the Adam-based model of the Garden of Eden, original sin, the sacrifice of innocent animals, and Jesus as the ultimate innocent sacrifice. A second Jesus-centric model focuses on what the Bible says Jesus claimed was most important. Instead of being driven by original sin, the Jesus-centric model views love as the greatest commandment. It further says love fulfills the law and focuses on not judging others but connecting with them, helping the least fortunate, forgiving people who have hurt us, and cultivating the kingdom within. The Jesus-centric model can be summed up in three words: love, connection, and service. The biblical justifications for both the Adam-based and Jesus-centric models are provided next.

In the Adam-based model, Jesus is the gatekeeper between God and humanity. In the Jesus-centric model, he provides an ongoing example for how Christians should live on earth—by loving God as the great *I AM* with all our hearts, loving our neighbors as ourselves, and helping others in need. Jesus did not write one word of the Bible, but what he did through the Bible was to help Christians see how to integrate humanity and divinity through his love for others, non-judgment of and connection to others, and feeding and healing those in need. For those deconstructing, compared to the Adam-based model, the Jesus-centric alternative prioritizes what Jesus did instead of what Adam did as the bedrock of the Christian faith. With this difference, the great commission need not be to convert nonbelievers but to love God and others as ourselves.

The Bible supports both Christian models. One highlights the sin-based dogma of the ancient Jews and the other the love-based priorities of Jesus in the New Testament. Adam-based believers can disagree with the Jesus-centric biblical interpretation, but they cannot say that the interpretation is not biblical, as highlighted through the side-by-side comparisons listed in Table 4.2, "Jesus-Centric vs. Adam-Based Christian Models."

Table 4.2. Jesus-Centric vs. Adam-Based Christian Models

JESUS-CENTRIC CHRISTIAN MODEL	ADAM-BASED CHRISTIAN MODEL
Jesus-centric Christianity based on the Bible	Adam-based Christianity based on the Bible
Love-based: Jesus prioritized love as the most important commandment (Matt. 22:36-40)	**Sin-based:** Adam ate fruit in the Garden of Eden, and all mankind was condemned because he did this (Gen. 3)
Forgiveness and non-judgment: Jesus preached perpetual forgiveness (Matt. 18:21-22) and taught that we should not judge others (Matt. 7:1-3)	**Judge others with no mercy:** God instructed Jews to judge and kill others for breaking rules, even including a death penalty for having unkempt hair (Lev. 10:6)
Compassion for the poor: Jesus had no personal financial assets (Matt. 8:20), and helped the least fortunate (John 8:7, Matt. 19:21)	**Prosperity rules:** God blessed his favorites with great wealth (2 Chron. 9:22) and gave them many wives and slaves (1 Kings 11:3)
Serving churches: Jesus vehemently opposed the corruption of the church and its leaders (Matt. 12:34)	**Powerful churches:** God created and empowered the church and its leaders (Numbers 18:21) and required blood sacrifices (1 Kings 8:63)
Religion killed Jesus: Jesus was killed by the corrupted church leaders (Matt. 12:14)	**Fruit killed Jesus:** Jesus was killed to make up for Adam eating the wrong fruit (Rom. 5:8, John 1:12)
Life happens now: Jesus said the kingdom was within (Luke 17:21) and to live in the present moment like the lilies (Matt. 6:28) and sparrows (Matt. 10:29-31)	**Life happens after death:** The kingdom is a physical place after we die for those who believe Adam-based dogma (Rev. 21:12-21) and say the sinner's prayer (not in Bible)

JESUS-CENTRIC CHRISTIAN MODEL	ADAM-BASED CHRISTIAN MODEL
Humanistic: Like Jesus, Christians can integrate humanity and divinity to love and help one another (James 2:14-17)	**Separatist:** Christians are soldiers, Jesus is the sword, and nonbelievers are the enemy (Matt. 10: 34-36)
Forgiving: Jesus forgave others and asked his followers to continually forgive others (Mark 11: 25-26)	**Selfish:** God only saves those who believe Adam-based dogma and accept Jesus as their savior (Eph. 2: 8-9)
Bring heaven to earth: Jesus prays for earth to be as it is in heaven (Matt. 6:10)	**Scorch the earth:** God scorches the earth to atone for the sin of Adam eating fruit once and for all (Rev. 20)
Non-dualistic interpretation of dogma overall	**Dualistic interpretation of dogma overall**
Unprovable dogma should not be interpreted literally	Unprovable dogma should be interpreted literally
The Bible is the history of the Judeo-Christian faith, to be lovingly celebrated	The Bible was essentially written by God, to be fearfully and literally followed
The focus of the church should be outside its sanctuary walls—to love, connect, and serve	The focus of the church should be inside its sanctuary walls—to obey, separate, and convert
Jesus-centric Christian model	**Adam-based Christian model**
Love Connection Service to the least fortunate Focused on life on earth	Judgment Separation Winner takes all Focused on life after death

The Biblical model we choose will affect how we deconstruct and live as Christians. It's not about whether the model is biblical or not. There are many ways to live Christian lives that are supported by the

Bible. Everyone cherry-picks Bible verses, whether they will admit it or not. What is critical is not so much what is in the Bible but how we choose to apply what is in the Bible. When deconstructing, legalistic dogma is not necessary unless it helps Christians love, connect, and serve. With a less dogmatic focus, we can transcend being like the blind guides who strain out gnats but swallow camels.[8]

Dogma does not need to be abandoned when using a Jesus-centric lens. Rather, it can be used in a richer way with less literalization and more spiritual context. We can embrace dogma as an important part of Christianity's history without needing to believe it is an immutable set of facts essentially written by an objectified God sitting on a throne, surrounded by mansions and streets of gold.

Many things do not need to change when transcending to a Jesus-centric model. The same Bible is the source of the faith's history and inspiration, Christian traditions are the same and still meaningful, and churches can continue to achieve great things for their members and local communities. Rather than disregarding the faith's traditions, we can enthusiastically honor our treasured history in more honest, loving, and spiritual ways.

Embracing a more Jesus-centric theological model can also help Christians who are more contemplative. Jesus said, "Neither will they say, 'Look, here!' or 'Look, there!' for behold, God's Kingdom is within you."[9] When deconstructing, shouldn't Jesus' life be the foundation of the Christian message? Jesus prioritized love, connection, and service over the Pharisees' model of legalism, separation, and judgment. Shouldn't that be the point?

While Jesus said that the truth will set us free,[10] truth will often make us uncomfortable first. The process requires that we unlearn certain things to learn other things and constantly improve through continuous deconstruction. This is needed for personal, spiritual, and congregational progress. Only a few hundred years ago, it was common for people to believe that humans caused earthquakes and that the earth was flat. By searching for greater truth through a

---

[8]Matt. 23:24

[9]Luke 17:21, WEB

[10]John 8:32

less-dogmatic and more Jesus-centric Christian faith, we can cultivate our intellectual and spiritual freedom, more honestly examine what we believe and why we believe, and discover how we can live better and more meaningful lives. We can turn Christianity from a faith we grow out of into a faith that we can grow into.

There is a lot that we do not understand, which is one reason why deconstruction is so important. With greater consciousness, Christians can learn much more from science. We can improve the Christian faith in the same way that scientists improve their fields of concentration, always regarding theories as approximations that are ready to be continually enhanced. Believing unprovable dogma is not a sign of faith: it is a refusal to pursue truth wherever it leads.

RETHINKING DOGMA

Christianity without literalistic dogma can give deconstructing Christians permission to say they do not know everything and do not need to know things that can't be proven by independent parties. We can believe things in a variety of ways without insisting that they are factual. Making supernatural things up to fill in knowledge gaps is neither healthy nor necessary. Instead, we can embrace not knowing as an important part of our spiritual journeys.

Through deconstruction, we can move beyond dogmatically imposed boundaries through constant curiosity and continuous exploration. We can crawl, then walk, and then run by learning, unlearning, and relearning how we can become more enlightened. The goal should not be to worship biblical dogma but to wisely use dogma to help us grow spiritually and in more Jesus-centric ways: through loving God and neighbors, being less judgmental, forgiving others, and serving people who are in need.

The religious elite in the New Testament didn't like the idea of love fulfilling the law because they made their livings teaching and defending the law. Christian dogma is to religious leaders today what the law was to the religious leaders in Jesus' time. Questioning dogma makes people mad now just like it did then because it threatens people who earn their livings because of it. The questions undermine their educational credentials, the stories they tell, and the livelihoods they depend upon.

In the social sciences, there are things known as *disorienting dilemmas*. They happen when someone's experience no longer aligns with what they believed was true and can only be resolved by changing their worldviews. When faced with disorienting dilemmas, people can drop out, put their heads in the sand, kill the messenger, or transform. Transformation is the hardest and almost always the best option.

Jesus introduced a disorienting dilemma to the religious elite in his day when he said that love fulfilled the law. Faced with this dilemma, the old guard was unwilling to transform and chose to kill the messenger. Imprisoned by their own legalism, the religious leaders in his day embraced a system of judgmentalism instead of love, separation instead of connection, and status-seeking instead of service to others. Jesus offered a different way. He did not preach from a mega-temple, nor did he hide away in a monastery or ashram. Jesus lived in the streets, helped and healed people who were suffering, and in so doing, made earth a little more like heaven.

With greater consciousness, Jesus spoke non-dualistically through his parables, beatitudes, and metaphorical arguments. He asked the religious elite to shed their legalism more than 2,000 years ago. Isn't what was true then even truer today? Christians could spend an entire lifetime focused only on the beatitudes and still never feel like they completed their spiritual journeys. Paul sums up conscious Christianity with three words: *Love fulfills law.* He wrote: "Whoever loves others has fulfilled the law. [...] Love is the fulfillment of the law."[11]

The Christian faith is at a crossroads. Dogma can either continue to undermine it or be used in a new way for a new time. There is a vast spiritual world on the other side of dogmatic literalism. Consider Jesus' miracles in the Bible. Isn't the greater truth to Christians today of Jesus feeding 5,000 people that he helped the hungry? Isn't the greater truth for communion not whether bread turns into flesh and wine into blood, but the connection of all things through love? Isn't the greater lesson from the sea

---

[11]Rom. 13:8,10 NIV

of Galilee that the roughest seas of people's lives can be calmed through faith? What if Christians could embrace the faith's timeless stories in new ways to live better lives, help the suffering, and create a better world?

Christians need not get trapped in the hornet's nest of dogmatic distraction. Why not simply embrace Jesus' highest priorities of love, connection, and service? Jesus said, "I am the light of the world. Whoever follows me will not walk in darkness but will have the light of life."[12] He said, "No man, when he has lit a candle, puts it in a secret place, neither under a bushel, but on a candlestick, that they which come in may see the light."[13] Jesus also said, "Ye are the light of the world. A city that is set on a hill cannot be hid."[14] Imagine if more than two billion Christians could individually see and then collectively become the light of the world through their love.

* * *

So far in this book, we have covered the three interdependencies of consciousness, religion, and dogma. The fourth interdependency in the Christian system is how organizational dynamics work. In many ways, this is one of the most powerful forces to understand when deconstructing how the Christian faith has worked throughout history, how it operates today, and how it can be transformed in the future. This is the subject of the next chapter.

CHAPTER SUMMARY IN STORYBOOK FORM

- Once upon a time, Christians believed that dogma was the foundation of their faith.
- Every day, they were taught to defend their dogma, all the way back to the original sin of Adam in the Garden of Eden.
- One day, they discovered that some of their dogma didn't add up and it made them act more like the Pharisees than Jesus.

---

[12]John 8:12, NIV

[13]Luke 11:33, RCV

[14]Matt. 5:14–15, KJV

- Because of that, they focused on what Jesus said was most important, not on things like what Adam ate in the Garden of Eden.
- Because of that, Christians began to embrace dogma in a more spiritual and Jesus-centric way.
- Until finally, they became more like Jesus—more loving, connecting, and serving.
- And then they were able to live happily ever after.

5

Fourth Interdependency: Organizations

Make a tree good and its fruit will be good, or make a tree bad and its fruit will be bad, for a tree is recognized by its fruit.

Matthew 12:33, NIV

ORGANIZATIONAL DYNAMICS ARE helpful to consider when deconstructing Christianity as a system because Christian dogma and organizational power are inextricably intertwined. In this sense, from a systems perspective, Christian denominations are like consumer product companies. Each has a differentiated message, a specific target audience, and requires organizational sales, recruitment, retention, delivery strategies and executional capabilities. These capabilities produce branded Christian experiences that are created through clearly defined organizational hierarchies that envision, design, build, and activate their dogmatic business models.

When social environments change, Christian and non-Christian organizations alike can either adapt or decline. The multi-generational drops in church attendance are symptomatic of a misalignment between old business models and new realities. Even though the overall Christian market is declining, like in business, a particular church can still grow at the expense of another by gaining market share. This has been the story of the Evangelical megachurch versus mainline Christian churches over the past few decades. However, megachurches will not be immune to the trends over time because markets always end up being more powerful than the organizations that serve them.

Christianity is a network of organizations. They need hierarchies to operate, the hierarchies concentrate organizational power, and greater organizational power eventually invites leadership corruption. In biblical times, Jesus stood up to the corrupt leaders of the Jewish hierarchy. They did not like him doing this, to the point where by aligning with politicians and local sympathizers, they used their power in ways that led to Jesus' death. Today, many Christian organizations are in a similar predicament. On one hand, they are attractive political voting blocs because members are inclined to do what their leaders tell them. But as churches have become more political, political values have been rebranded as Christian values, and the moral compass of modern Christianity has been lost in the translation.

One characteristic that *is* unique to religious organizations versus secular consumer products companies is the ability for dogmatic leaders to manipulate their members by using supernaturalism and making things up in real time by speaking for God through prophetic *words of knowledge*. These proclamations, claimed to be coming from God, can be scary, hateful, and are conveniently used to extort people's money.

Calling opinions "prophecies" does not increase their accuracy. The New York Times researched a predominant charismatic publisher. After publishing thousands of claims that Donald Trump was divinely anointed by God, would win the 2020 election, and was sent by God to wage war against destructive spirits, the publisher finally had to admit that it got things wrong. Yet, after all of this, the CEO affirmed that the overall editorial approach wouldn't change. "No," he said. "We won't back off from the prophets."[1]

*   *   *

Christian beliefs can be traced back to the organizations that created and institutionalized them. These organizations have cultivated Christian dogma in a way that helps to sustain their business models. The dogma can't be tampered with very much because of this. So, for example, if a leader is speaking on behalf of a Southern Baptist organization, regardless of what their personal beliefs might be in private, they will be obligated to preach Southern Baptist dogma. If they don't, the organization will ensure they will not stray twice.

Christianity is a big business and a significant political force. According to IBISWorld research, Christianity has revenues of about $124 billion per year and employs around two million people in the United States alone. Main players in the U.S. include Catholic, Evangelical, and mainline Protestant churches. In addition to a vast supply chain of pastors and priests, many support organizations exist, including musical groups and artists, caterers, land leasing firms, janitorial services, media companies, and uniform manufacturers and distributors. The ecosystem is further supported by a large network of schools, universities, seminaries, youth organizations, adult retreats, church planters, and motivational speakers.[2] I refer to this ecosystem as Christianity, Inc. in this book. Of course, as in the secular world, every one of these organizations needs to earn money through donations, paid invoices, or a combination of the two.

There would not be more than two billion Christians today if it were not for Christianity, Inc. As noted in Chapter 3, "Religion: Second Interdependency," organizations are required to help religions scale. While Christianity, Inc. is obviously uniquely Christian, the organizations themselves—individually and collectively—are

---

[1] Quoted in Sam Kestenbaum's "For Trump Prophets, Life and Book Sales Go On," *New York Times*, September 20, 2021.

[2] Anna Miller, "Religious Organizations in the US—From the pulpit: Renewed incomes are expected to boost donations, but attendance will likely continue declining," US Industry (NAICS) Report 81311, August 2020. IBIS-World. https://www.ibisworld.com/united-states/market-research-reports/religious-organizations-industry/

fundamentally structured like every other business, non-profit, and government entity.

All organizations need to differentiate themselves to be successful. For more than 1,000 years, this Christian differentiation occurred through the Catholic Church, prior to the split-off of Eastern Orthodox Christianity in the 11th century. Then, the Protestant reformation expanded the market in the 16th century through further differentiation. Given that Protestants were not centrally controlled by a Pope-like leader, various new organizations emerged with additional dogmatic twists. In the 20th century, megachurches became more prominent in the United States, and celebrity minister-communicators and Christian radio and television personalities became more prevalent.

Churches are the basic operating units of Christianity, Inc., but they are only one part of the system. To illustrate, consider that in non-religious organizations, there are boards that control strategy, product developers who position what is sold, salespeople who get customers to buy, and relationship managers who keep customers engaged. In Christianity, denominations are like the boards setting strategy, apologists are like product developers (responsible for positioning and defending the denomination's dogma); bishops, cardinals, evangelists, and megachurch communicators are like salespeople; and local pastors and priests are like relationship managers.

Like every other organization, churches need to provide a service, generate revenue, manage expenses, and be organizationally led and sustained. The organizations themselves are designed to first survive and ideally grow. If churches are super successful at growing their members and revenues, their leaders will become tempted to further consolidate their power. This consolidated power can often lead to increased organizational corruption.

Bad practices are the fruit of bad organizations. Churches have traumatized many, making Christian deconstruction emotionally difficult for members and ex-members, especially women, black and other people of color, and non-heterosexuals. One source of trauma is churches' systematic use of fear-based dogma to recruit and retain members. Additionally, that dogma may be used to keep members from marrying outside their faith and encourage high birth rates to increase the flock. Religious practices like these go back as far as the Levites prior to Moses.

In the same way business schools prepare young adults to manage companies, Christian denominations use seminaries as dogmatic feeder systems to run churches. There, future ministers learn their denomination's approaches for interpreting scripture, pastoral care, preaching, and church administration. They are taught to explain and defend their dogma and help their churches scale their own messages, cultures, and belief systems. Dogmatic beliefs in churches are like brands in companies. If you buy a Coke in Dallas, it will be like the Coke you buy in Atlanta. It is the same if you attend a Catholic parish or Southern Baptist church in both cities: You can rely on the brand, regardless of the location. If this didn't happen, these organizations wouldn't be able to scale.

In some ways, Christianity, Inc. is like an organizational vending machine. Overall, it seems to represent one Christian faith, but it is filled with many brands to choose from, each promising consumers that it is the best choice. Different churches provide different branded experiences from this vending machine, including ritualists, fundamentalists, liberals, charismatics, and prosperity thinkers. Some churches like it quiet, and others do not mind you dancing on the pews. Some churches pay their pastors well, while others provide mere subsistence. Some are political; others are not. Some play the supernatural card heavily, others not as much. But what is similar across them is that they are all organizations with well-defined hierarchies designed to recruit and retain members, collect revenues, and manage expenses.

ORGANIZATIONAL HIERARCHIES

Organizations are designed to achieve things that their members cannot achieve as individuals. They require organizational hierarchies to do this, and these hierarchies can be used for good as well as evil. This has nothing to do with whether the organization is Christian or non-Christian. All organizational hierarchies concentrate power, and ultimately it is the leaders who choose what to do with this power. ⁷ (An additional byproduct of hierarchical power is its propensity to cultivate hero worship at the top.) Followers are usually inclined to believe what their organization's leaders say and are typically willing, and even eager, to act according to their wishes. While there are bad leaders in Christian organizations, their corruption is not caused by Christianity any more than bank robbers are caused by the banking system.

One caveat is that while power corrupts irrespective of organizational type, dogma can make corruption worse in religious organizations because leaders can play the supernatural card. In secular organizations, leaders do not claim to speak for God, proclaim God's favor, warn of Satan's demonic interference, or promise miracles. Something common in *both* secular and religious organizations is that greater organizational success will often increase leadership hubris.

Sometimes, organizational power combined with supernatural dogma can develop cult-like environments and even full-fledged cults. Members will often join a group thinking that it is good, find it personally beneficial for a while, and then get increasingly trapped in the dogmatic webs that its organizational leaders have constructed. Today, we sadly have the expression "drink the Kool-Aid" because Reverend Jim Jones, leader of the People's Temple of the Disciples of Christ, had the power to orchestrate a mass suicide and murder more than 900 people, including more than 300 children, in Jonestown, Guyana. Dogma and hierarchical power can be a dangerous combination. As soon as members believe something that is not provable because organizational leaders say it is true, they stop trusting in their own judgment. Once they are willing to stop trusting their own judgment, they are primed to be manipulated.

Cults, even non-religious ones, share some common traits: members are often manipulated by leaders and peers into believing that they are special, they are encouraged to recruit additional members, there is usually a specific transformation and indoctrination process, and members are often encouraged to increase their levels of commitment and separate from others over time. Another common ingredient of cults is the use of peer pressure and exploiting personal vulnerability as means of control. For example, the NXIVM cult required women to provide embarrassing "collateral" material to the organization. Scientology does this by collecting information gathered during "auditing" sessions. The Catholic Church does this through "confessions," and evangelicals ask people to publicly admit their transgressions through public testimonies.

Independent governance practices help organizations avoid the dysfunctions of hierarchical corruption in public companies, including public disclosure of management compensation and perks and the use of internal and external auditors to verify organizational honesty. Churches owe their members the same because poor transparency often encourages bad behaviors. Without a culture of transparency, terrible things can happen. Consider the horrific cases of pedophilia that have been discovered across many otherwise secretive Christian denominations, including the Catholic Church, Jehovah's Witnesses, Children of God, and the fundamentalist Church of Jesus Christ of Latter-Day Saints. The lack of organizational transparency combined with supernaturally-enhanced belief systems can make poorly led churches particularly corrupt and abusive places.

ORGANIZATIONAL BUSINESS MODELS

Business models are the underlying rationale for how organizations create, deliver, and capture value. In this context, Christianity, Inc., which is a large collection of business models that all profess to support Jesus Christ, is a significant organizational achievement. The Catholic Church was the world's first global organization, and many other Christian organizations are impressive in their size and reach. Given the extensive nature of Christianity's infrastructure, the good that Christianity can do is incalculable. Yet for many of the reasons already mentioned, this capability can be used for good and ill.

In rapidly changing markets, organizations can either adapt their business models or stand by and watch their business decline. Christianity has been around for millennia and has a long history of adaptation, as far back as Paul's letters in the New Testament.

Paul was deliberately building a new Judaic business model for the 1st century. He expanded the existing market to include Gentiles by deemphasizing the Jewish diet and dropping the requirement for male circumcision. He also helped build the next generation of churches by using people's homes instead of temples, ensuring that expenses did not exceed revenues.

Today, according to the National Congregations Study published in *Christianity Today*, there are more than 300,000 churches across 200 denominations in the United States alone.[3] Each of these 300,000 organizations has a business model to help it survive and try to thrive. They all have markets to serve, revenue to generate, and expenses to control.

As a business consultant, I have often watched leaders of established organizations adopt an "If it ain't broke, don't fix it" attitude. They naturally want to continue using what has worked in the past. Leaders will often yearn for the good old days when their business models were better aligned to the market. Unfortunately for leaders who think this way, history has consistently shown that new environments are usually far more powerful than old business models. For example, in the secular retail industry in the 20th century, Woolworth did not break away from Main Street when Sears entered the malls. Kmart took over from Sears with its deep discount, city orientation. It was then unable to beat Walmart when Sam Walton moved in from the rural areas. Amazon changed everything again. Deliberate adaptation to changing environments always prevails, which is why industry leaders typically get disrupted by start-ups with a fraction of their resources.

Transforming organizational business models is not trivial. As organizations grow, they lose flexibility and need to stay consistent with their brands and standardized operations. A small, independent hamburger stand can procure ingredients and cook up a burger any way the chef wants. McDonald's cannot. A preacher on a street corner can say anything he or she wants; the Pope cannot. As organizations

---

[3]Rebecca Randall, "How Many Churches Does America Have? More Than Expected," Christianity Today (*Christianity Today*, September 14, 2017), https://www.christianitytoday.com/news/2017/september/how-many-churches-in-america-us-nones-nondenominational.html.

scale, overhead increases, and these costs need to be covered through increased revenues. The need for more revenue requires churches to keep the members they have while still attracting new ones. Yet in changing environments, the new members often want different things than the current members do. This situation can be difficult to manage.

The Evangelical alliance has become very powerful over the past 50 years. Some Evangelical leaders may wish to believe that this has been due to God's blessing, but evangelicalism has simply had a more innovative and politically savvy business model during this time. The Evangelical business model was put on the map in the 20th century by gifted communicators like Billy Graham and Billy Sunday before him. Evangelical crusades provided an emotionally exciting, fear-based, easy-to-understand admission policy: get attendees to say the sinner's prayer due to the fear of hell and provide a ready-made network of conservative churches for converts to attend after the crusades were over.

Organizations are known by their fruit. Bad business models eventually keep organizations from being able to live up to their own standards. If you are deconstructing, consider reflecting upon how your church is doing with respect to delivering on core Jesus-centric values like loving neighbors, practicing non-judgment and forgiveness, and helping people in need.

There has also always been a political and populist element of Evangelical success. Billy Sunday dined with numerous politicians, including presidents Theodore Roosevelt and Woodrow Wilson, and he counted both Herbert Hoover and John D. Rockefeller, Jr. as friends. Billy Graham was also very well connected. He was a spiritual adviser to U.S. presidents and provided spiritual counsel for every president, from Harry S. Truman (33rd) to Barack Obama (44th). Since then, political connections have rapidly swung further to the right and in more data-driven ways.

Building upon its historical use of flamboyant communicators, the Evangelical megachurch has scaled Evangelical tent and stadium theatrics at the local level in a repeatable way over the past 40 years. The multi-campus megachurch became technically enabled by concert-quality sound and video systems that continued to leverage the talents of world-class communicators.

Like other successful companies, successful megachurches have been world-class sales organizations, and smaller, mainline Protestant and Catholic churches have struggled to compete in their shadows. This is no different from how shopping malls impacted locally-owned downtown stores in the 1970s and how malls themselves have been weakened by the rise of online shopping.

No business model lasts forever. So, can megachurches go the way of the shopping mall? A more reasonable question might be, why wouldn't they? The dogma that helped sustain Christian churches in the 20th century now seems to be accelerating their declines, and megachurches aren't immune from this effect. The internet and social media changed everything. Dogma works better when there aren't dissenting voices, but it does not work as well when every member has unlimited access to independent information. Before the web and social media, church leaders could easily control the dialog, use their dogma to scare people into submission, and claim that their church or theology provided God's one true way. This has not been the case for quite some time.

Using prayer as a means of control is also losing its power. Younger people are not as easily convinced when Christian leaders use their spoken prayers to play the supernatural card and claim to speak on God's behalf. With generations of people increasingly not believing the unprovable, dogmatic leaders are finding it more difficult to use their spoken prayers to manipulate congregational thinking, sell prayer cloths over network television, or ask for private jets to help them spread "the word of the Lord."

It's getting harder to convince people with rhetoric like, "If you get healed, *praise God*. If you do not, *God must have had other plans*. But thanks for the money, anyway." Using dogma to manipulate poor people into giving money that they do not have in exchange for benefits that cannot be guaranteed is no longer a sustainable business model. Likewise, the use of special "words of knowledge" to scare audiences into digging deeper into their wallets is imploding on itself. Given how enraged Jesus was with the money changers in the temple, it's hard to imagine how angry he would have been had he lived amongst some of today's Christian leaders.

When deconstructing, it may be useful to examine your church's business model, starting with assessing your church leader on the following points:

- Where Jesus prioritized love over law and asked for people to live lives of non-judgment, is your church leader unloving and judgmental?
- Where Jesus modeled service for the least fortunate and turning the other cheek, does your church leader demonstrate self-indulgence and judge people who are different?
- Where Jesus said the truth would set people free, does your church leader use and militarize unprovable dogma to control members through fear, uncertainty, and doubt?
- Where Jesus said the meek shall inherit the earth, does your church leader, funded by tithes and offerings, live a lifestyle significantly more lavish than the church members?

THE INDUSTRIALIZED LAMB

The term *military-industrial complex* refers to an alliance between the nation's military and the defense industry that supplies it. It is a sophisticated way to say that the parties are in cahoots. Over the centuries, Christianity has industrialized in similar ways. One of the most important examples occurred in AD 313 when Constantine embraced Christianity throughout the Roman Empire via the Edict of Milan. Eventually, many countries officially recognized Christianity as their national faith, often including government funding for state churches. The United States, alternatively, was founded on the principle of separating church and state. When the church and state combine, political *and* religious organizational corruption usually seems to follow.

Despite the separation of church and state, as with the military-industrial complex, right-wing Christian Nationalism has increased in the United States. Secularist Americans—whose positions have been closer to the intents of the founding fathers—have consistently been politically and culturally squelched.

Katherine Stewart researched the history of Christian Nationalism and the motives of the power brokers behind the movement. In *The Power Worshippers*, she writes:

> The leaders of the movement have demonstrated real savvy in satisfying some of the emotional concerns of their followers, but they have little intention of giving them a voice in where the movement is going. [...] It is a means through which a small number of people, quite a few of them residing in the Washington D.C. area, harness the passions, resentments, and insecurities of a large and diverse population in their own quest for power. [...] The leaders of the movement have quite consciously reframed the Christian religion itself to suit their political objectives, thus turning citizens into congregants and congregants into voters.[4]

Being a nation full of Christians is great, but insisting that the United States is a Christian nation is un-American. The difference between being a Christian nation and a nation that protects the freedoms of Christians and other citizens is a difference worthy of serious reflection.

A problem when Christian organizations become political is that by doing this, they often become less Jesus-centric. When religion and politics mix, politics always seems to end up leading the dance, contrary to Jesus' admonition to give unto Caesar what is Caesar's.[5] As an obvious example, it's curious how churches, which themselves depend upon tax-exempt status, can so easily preach with righteous indignation against redistributing wealth to the poor through taxes. The separation of church and state in the United States is foundational

---

[4]Katherine Stewart, *The Power Worshippers: Inside the Dangerous Rise of Religious Nationalism.* Read by Tosca Hopkins. New York: Bloomsbury, 2020.

[5]Luke 20:25

to the country's democracy. This status is what is supposed to differentiate the U.S. from theocracies like Iran and Afghanistan.

Religiously charged politics does not lead to good places. We saw examples on September 11th, 2001 from Islamic radicals in New York, Pennsylvania, and Washington D.C., and on January 6th, 2021 in Washington D.C. by Christian radicals. These are unfortunately not the only examples, even by Americans. There have been many documented acts of murder, attempted murder, assault, kidnapping, arson, bombing, anthrax threats, and property crime at family planning clinics by radical Christian groups, including one interestingly calling itself the *Army of God.*[6]

The way we look at things often changes how things look. It is in this sense that hateful people predictably produce hateful versions of Christianity. For example, an important part of the Christian deconstruction movement focuses on the ruthless colonization acts of straight white males over the centuries. There have been many examples throughout history, including colonization with the intent of wealth extraction in much of the world, the Christian Crusades from 1095-1291, and the Thirty Years' War in the 13th and 17th centuries. In the United States, the Ku Klux Klan itself was first rooted in local Protestant communities seeking to maintain white supremacy and oppose Catholics and Jews, leading to Jim Crow era laws, burning crosses in yards, and inflicting many documented and who knows how many undocumented racially-motivated lynchings.

Due to a relatively small number of powerful but corrupt religious and political leaders working in cahoots, the brands of the Evangelical church and the Republican party will probably never be untarnished. Together, they seem to be increasingly being reframed as the crazy, male-dominated, white supremacist, flat-earth folks who stormed the Capitol building. Behind the scenes, political conservatives become more radical as moderates leave, conservative Christians seem to be becoming more political, both are becoming more desperate, and the result seems to be the rapid formation of a new Christian Nationalist party. Meanwhile, Christian church attendance declines. As right-wing Christians and the Republican party become allies, the integrity of

---

[6]"Anti-abortion violence," March 23, 2021, https://en.wikipedia.org/wiki/Anti-abortion_violence#United_States.

centrist Christian faith has suffered collateral damage. Deconstruction is one sign, and there will likely be others, of the moderate majority becoming more vocal.

ORGANIZATIONS CREATE DOGMA

Dogma is not divine truth created through supernatural forces. Instead, it is a theological product envisioned, designed, built, and activated by religious organizations. This is especially true with traditional Christianity because unlike Muhammad and the *Quran*, Joseph Smith and the *Book of Mormon*, and L. Ron Hubbard and *Dianetics*, there are no direct writings from Jesus as the founder of the faith.

The source of Christian dogma is usually the Bible, but Christian organizations tend to use the Bible in a meta-dogmatic way, making it difficult to deconstruct. For example, unprovable dogma is used to position the Bible as supernatural, and then that positioning is used to justify the unprovable dogma inside it. This results in many circular theological debates. Christians claim that something is true because it is in the Bible and that this can't be challenged because they have also claimed the Bible is the unchallengeable word of God. This leads to a never-ending series of unprovable dogmatic rabbit holes.

Meta-dogma is a problem outside of traditional Christianity as well. For example, consider the golden plates in Mormonism. Joseph Smith claimed to have found golden plates near his home in Manchester, New York, in 1823. Directed by the angel he named Moroni, Smith said he translated those plates from an ancient language into the *Book of Mormon*, published in 1830. Eleven of Smith's friends vouched for him. Smith said he returned the plates back to the angel Moroni, thereby removing all the evidence.

The Bible itself did not magically appear on people's nightstands. Oral traditions were written down and collected. In the case of the Christian Bible, after thousands of years of work by Jewish and Catholic scribes, theologians, and committees, today's Bible was formalized. The starting point for the Christian Bibles that Protestants, Catholics, and Mormons use today was the Jewish canonization process, largely completed by the 1st century BC. The Christian canonization process was mainly complete by the 4th century, and the Catholic Bible began to take form about 500 years after the time of Christ. The Catholic Church determined its content and how it should be used. At that point, there was essentially one Church, one Bible, and one official form of Christian dogma.

About 1,000 years later, the leaders of the Protestant Reformation challenged the authority of the Catholic Church, and then Luther produced a German version of the Bible in the 1500s before the King James English Bible was published for the public in 1611. Protestants were not constrained by Catholic Church doctrine. They were free to interpret the Bible in an unmediated way, albeit guided by the heavy hands of denominational leaders, including Martin Luther and John Calvin. As Protestantism expanded, different Christian organizations produced different dogmatic models. Today, Christian Protestants come in a variety of flavors, all claiming that their way is the best way. For deconstructing Christians worried about questioning their one true way, don't worry: the short list of "best ways" includes those of the Adventists, Anabaptists, Anglicans, Episcopalians, Baptists, Calvinists, Evangelicals, Lutherans, Methodists, Pentecostals, Charismatics, Presbyterians, Quakers, and many independents.

DECONSTRUCTING IN REAL LIFE: *"I have served in professional pastoral roles for over 20 years and have been the senior pastor at my church of 50–60 members for 12 years. For me, deconstruction came from deeper study of the Bible. My deconstruction is still unfolding. I am doing a lot of unlearning and unteaching."*

Because of these organizational influences, it is foolish to ask, "What does the Bible say?" and wiser to ask, "How can the Bible best be used to love God and others?" As will be described in the next section, the Bible is not so much a supernaturally created document as it is an organizational platform that can be interpreted in various ways. The Bible contains many documents related to the early history of Judaism and Christianity. This is in and of itself quite remarkable, and the fact that more than two billion people basically share the same

Bible might even qualify as something like an eighth wonder of the world. No literalistic beliefs in church dogma are needed to view the Bible as the history of the Christian faith, and this in and of itself is truly beautiful and remarkable.

As I deconstructed personally, I fell in love with the fact that the Bible contained thousands of years of Christian and Judaic writings that could come alive when I didn't need to believe that God supernaturally wrote it or that I needed to relate every verse to every other verse. I was able to better appreciate how various writers thought, learn ancient cultural beliefs, and I was free to read with horror about the many ancient atrocities that occurred, such as murder, genocide, slavery, looting, human rights abuses, and several cruel punishments that were put in place for bizarre infractions. The Bible is a potpourri of our faith's history. In it, God is described in a variety of ways, the earth is believed to be flat, and because the earth is believed to be flat, heaven is conceptualized as above and hell below. And of course, the list goes on and has been argued over for many centuries.

Independent people can agree on a lot about the Bible if dogma is not required to be interpreted literally. For example, it is not controversial to accept that Paul was a central writer of the New Testament who never met Jesus. Also, he seemed to be instrumental in building the early Christian church since about 30% of the New Testament consists of letters he wrote. Paul naturally carried forward a lot of Jewish doctrine into his writings as a trained Pharisee. His letters reveal a desire to consolidate Christianity under the Jewish idea of one true God but in a more culturally flexible way. Paul tried to balance what Gentiles could embrace with what Jews could understand.

The Bible is a priceless history of the Christian faith, largely integrated by the Catholic Church many centuries ago. How Christians use it today is like a religious Rorschach test, telling us more about who is reading the Bible than the Bible that is being read. Deconstructing Christians have many choices on how to read the Bible: its dogma can be seen as literal or historical, it can be seen as Adam-based or Jesus-centric, or it can inspire people to hate or love.

Biblical authors had their own cultural influences over thousands of years and their own purposes for writing what they did. The Jewish and Catholic scribes who assembled the writings into what became the Bible had their own motives as well. One can only guess the nature of all these motives. It is not hard to imagine Moses using his ruthless descriptions of God to try to control and unify the tribes of Israel, or David revving up his soldiers to win battles by killing men, women, and children in the name of a higher power. Is it impossible that someone would do all of this in the name of almighty God? Of course not. Pope Urban II did the same thing 1,000 years after the time of Christ when he called Christians in Europe to engage in war against Muslims, promising spiritual rewards for their efforts on God's behalf.

THE BIBLE IS AN ORGANIZATIONAL PLATFORM

A *platform* is a technical environment for building, tailoring, and running applications, systems, and processes. The Bible is used in this way by Christian organizations, with the same Bible tailored in a variety of ways by different denominations, churches, and Christian speakers and authors. For example, the Bible was first used by the Catholic Church as a platform for training priests and church members, establishing rules, and creating rituals over many centuries.

DECONSTRUCTING IN REAL LIFE: *"After studying the Bible in Christian college and seminary, I found it increasingly stopped making sense. As my questions increased, they were dismissed. The mental gymnastics became too tiring. The theology I grew up with was toxic. When questions could not be answered, the default response was, "Don't question God." To coexist with others, I had to increasingly focus on less and less of the Bible and what the church taught, and I didn't want to pretend anymore."*

Interpreting the Bible is a corporate matter for Catholics, whereas it is more of a denominational choice for Protestants. With Catholics, Jesus died for everyone, very few go to hell, and if they do, that decision is left up to God. With fundamentalist Christians, everyone goes to hell if they have not accepted Jesus into their hearts. Other Protestant churches—because there is no centralized control across them—have a variety of biblical belief systems. The gamut runs from ritualistic churches, like Episcopal churches, to churches where members dance with poisonous snakes as they cling to a saying attributed to Jesus—that followers "will pick up snakes with their hands, and if they drink any deadly poison, it will not harm them."[7] This is another example of why literally interpreting the Bible is sometimes not a good idea.

Dogma is difficult to challenge within denominations and churches because it is often hard-wired into their business platforms. For example, even if an Assemblies of God minister wanted to denounce inerrancy, they would not be free to do so because the belief is so strongly embedded in the Assemblies of God platform. The dogmatic wiring is embedded throughout a wide range of practices, seminaries, curricula, public statements, media vehicles, political committees, and the hearts and minds of its members. However, even for very dogmatic churches, improvements are possible. Churches can continue to believe in their dogma 100%, yet still position their beliefs in a more Jesus-centric way. Every church can strive to be 10% more loving, less judgmental, more forgiving, and helpful to people in need. No dogma prevents any of this.

Deconstructing the Bible can be approached in a fairly straightforward way despite all of the emotion, judgment, mumbo jumbo, and hocus-pocus that often lurks in the background. To begin, one can consider three major options. At the highest level, the Bible can be (a) 100% false, (b) 100% factual, or (c) something in between.

Consider:

100% False: Even atheists don't truly believe this. If someone claims the Bible is 100% false, the person will have to believe that *none* of the historical figures in the Bible ever existed, that every bit of history in the Old and New Testaments is made up, and that there is nothing objectively valuable in the Bible from cover to cover. One would have to conclude that Jesus—and everyone else in the Bible, for that matter—never existed and therefore could not have had anything important to say. If the Bible is 100% false, one's conclusion would need to be that what is in the Bible has never and will never

---

[7] Mark 16:18, NASB

have anything to offer humanity other than falsehoods, even as a book of fables.

100% Factual: Even fundamentalists don't truly believe this. If the Bible is 100% factual, there is no wiggle room to reject any verse in it; otherwise, one would have to choose the "something in-between" category. With the "God wrote it," 100% factual option, someone will have to believe or explain all of the following:

- In Genesis 1, that we live in a 6,000-year-old universe;
- In Genesis 4, since Adam and Eve were the first humans, that Cain's wife had to be his sister;
- In Genesis 6, that two of every creature (from dinosaurs, elephants, and lions to gnats and mosquitoes) were caught, placed, lived, and remained on a 75-foot-wide boat and lived, ate, and relieved themselves in one place in perfect health and harmony, floating on an entirely flooded earth for 40 days and 40 nights;
- That God condones polygamy beginning in Genesis 26 and slaves beginning in Exodus 21—and continues to do so throughout the Bible;
- That God demanded that large numbers of innocent animals be sacrificed beginning in Exodus 29 (and in extremely large numbers with Solomon sacrificing 144,000 sheep and cattle in 1 Kings);
- That God cannot control his own temper, as he says in Exodus 33, and shows his thirst for blood throughout the Old Testament, as he kills hundreds of thousands of men, women, and children, even though *not* killing is one of the Ten Commandments in Exodus 20;
- And that establishing the death penalty for many infractions, including torn clothes, was appropriate in Leviticus 10.

To add a couple of things (certainly not a comprehensive list) from the New Testament, 100% literalists will have to believe that it is right to pluck out one's own eye if it causes them to sin (Matthew 5), that the book of Revelation literally reveals that the earth is flat, that the moon is a source of light, that the sun and moon orbit around the earth, and that the stars are fixed and near enough to quickly plunge to the earth.

If someone can't sign up for the Bible being 100% false or 100% factual, then the only option left is that the Bible is something in between the two.

Something In Between: In a 2017 Gallup poll, only 24% of Christians reported they believed in Biblical inerrancy.[8] This number has continually declined over the years. Practically speaking, even the most fundamentalist churches pick and choose for some of the reasons previously listed. It's simply a matter of what and why they pick and choose based on the underlying model (as described in Chapter 4) that they use to organize their biblical interpretations.

> **DECONSTRUCTING IN REAL LIFE:** *"I deconstructed after college while actively raising support to become a missionary. It has been about 2–3 years since then, and I still hold a job in the church (I wanted to finish out my commitment—I have 2 years left). My biggest struggles have been fear of others discovering what I really believe and to continue to work for an institution I don't align with anymore."*

Inerrant literalization limits the Bible's potential for Christians to focus on Jesus' priorities of love, non-judgment, forgiveness, and serving those in need. A more conscious option is to embrace the Bible as a treasured history of the faith shared by more than two billion people worldwide. Without literalistic dogma, the Bible can be objectively embraced by Christians and non-Christians alike as a historical treasure. It is the result of an incalculable amount of effort of both transmission and preservation over thousands of years, arguably more than any other book in human history.

Embracing the Bible as the history of the Christian faith can expand its spiritual impact. The Bible is filled with verses that can

---

[8]Lydia Saad, "Record Few Americans Believe Bible Is Literal Word of God," Gallup.com (Gallup, March 23, 2021), https://news.gallup.com/poll/210704/record-few-americans-believe-bible-literal-word-god.aspx.

help Christians and non-Christians alike more consciously create better lives and a better world. Christians do not have to get trapped in the theological dilemma of trying to explain how every Bible verse relates to every other Bible verse in support of their denominational business models. The Bible's contents were not written to be read as a single body of work. Turning the Bible into an end-to-end, dogmatically literal manifesto is as emotionally exhausting as it is intellectually futile.

The Christian fundamentalist slogan, "The Bible says it, I believe it, that settles it," is in the Dictionary of Christianese and has been frequently cited over the past 60 years.[9] But this slogan is not helpful to the Christian faith for many reasons highlighted in this chapter. Many deconstructing Christians know in their hearts that love is the right answer but struggle because the dogma they have been taught is like a minefield of hate and dogmatic contradictions. The gnats have overtaken the camels. If the interactions between Jesus and the religious elite in the Bible demonstrate anything, it is how arguing about religious doctrine occurs at the expense of love as Christianity's greatest commandment.

* * *

The Bible is a Christian treasure, but the compulsion to turn it into a business platform is unwise. The Bible can speak to Christians and non-Christians alike with no need for literalistic dogma. It can be read and reflected upon with the same love, care, and emotional attachment we give to our treasured family photos, filled with precious moments, landmark events, and bad haircuts.

Even the Book of Revelation, often the ultimate crowd-pleaser for the fear-based fundamentalist business model, provides important allegorical insights, including a very conscious and transcendent narrative for rebirth with the lamb overcoming the beast, the transformation of humanity, and a new heaven and new earth taking place in people's hearts and minds.

---

[9]Tim Stewart, "God Said It, I Believe It, That Settles It," *Dictionary of Christianese* (Dictionary of Christianese, August 19, 2013), https://www.dictionaryofchristianese.com/god-said-it-i-believe-it-that-settles-it/.

Dogmatic problems in Christianity do not exist because of the Bible but because of how Christian organizations have chosen to use the Bible. Christians can use the Bible more consciously and constructively if they choose to do so. It does not have to be seen as a set of ancient commands from a sovereign and judgmental God on a throne. The Bible can also be embraced as a shared history of the faith to help billions of people individually and collectively live better and more loving lives.

So far, we have covered the four Christian system interdependencies of consciousness, religion, dogma, and organizations. So, we come now to the fifth interdependency and the subject of the next chapter: a way to deconstruct the nature of God.

CHAPTER SUMMARY IN STORYBOOK FORM

- Once upon a time, Christians thought church organizations functioned differently from other organizations.
- Every day, they trusted their leaders to tell them the truth and look out for their spiritual interests.
- One day, they discovered that Christian organizations, like the temples that angered Jesus in the New Testament, were capable of harm.
- Because of that, they became more aware of the pitfalls that could come from organizational hierarchy, power, corruption, and greed.
- Because of that, they also saw that the Bible and dogma were sometimes used as organizational weapons.
- Until finally, they were able to deconstruct their Christian faith to live more loving and abundant lives.
- And then they were able to live happily ever after.

6

Fifth Interdependency: The Godhead

In the beginning was the Word, and the Word was with God, and the Word was God.

John 1:1

GOD IS THE fifth interdependency in the *Christianity without Dogma* analysis because it is the most difficult to deconstruct and significantly influenced by the preceding four interdependencies. How people conceptualize God is affected by the dualistic and non-dualistic thinking they have adopted (as part of the consciousness interdependency), the way they have embraced religion versus spirituality, the Christian dogma they have been taught, and how they have been directly impacted by organizations within Christianity, Inc.

The subject of God can be both touchy and confusing. Imagine asking three friends to give you their definitions of God. Even agreeing on a construct to begin the conversation would be challenging. Is God the creator of the universe? Universal intelligence? A man-like being on a throne? Vengeful? Loving? Physical? Spiritual? A single entity? Three entities in one? Does God exist at all?

Now, imagine asking billions of people to define God. While this would be impossible, religious leaders frequently define God with great clarity and certainty, denominationally packaging God Almighty as crisply as a bar of soap, or like the three-legged Father, Son, and Holy Spirit stool.

Christians are taught dualistic definitions of God the Father because the idea of a sovereign being is relatively easy to conceptualize. It is simple for children and adults alike to think about God in this way. When things are going well, the man in the sky is obviously taking good care of us. Good things become "God things." But the micromanaging man-in-the-sky characterization can also be problematic. Did you find a parking space? God must have known you were running late. Did you lose a child? Well, God must have a better plan. A sovereign God is easy to conceptualize, but the model does not generally hold up well when someone is deconstructing.

Christians do not need to put God into an oversimplified dogmatic box. Using the same Bible, if someone chooses, they can embrace God in a less dualistic and more spiritual way. God can also exist contemplatively in the present moment—or as the Bible says, as the great *I Am*.[1]

* * *

The dogma that churches use to define God is integrated into their business models. God is typically described dualistically and denominationally branded, defended, and monetized. But how deconstructing Christians define God is a choice. Using the same Bible, God can be defined both dualistically and non-dualistically. Consider the definitions in Table 6.1, "How Do You Define God?"

---

[1] See Exod. 3:14

Table 6.1—How Do You Define God?

Four Interdependencies	Dualistic Image	Non-Dualistic Image
First Interdependency (Consciousness)	**Dualistic:** As the man-like being described in the Bible	**Non-Dualistic:** As the great *I Am*, spirit, and love described in the Bible
Second Interdependency (Religion)	**Religious:** As the religious, legalistic, and jealous being in the Bible	**Spiritual:** As the loving, spiritual, and mysterious force in the Bible
Third Interdependency (Dogma)	**Corporate:** As an unchanging being in the Bible who is not to be dogmatically challenged over the ages	**Personal:** As a living, omnipresent force in the Bible, beyond being able to be put into a dogmatic box
Fourth Interdependency (Organization)	**Packaged:** Officially defined and spoken for, on behalf of the church using the Bible	**Emergent:** Personally experienced through contemplation

(handwritten margin note: God is still speaking)

When people claim to believe or not believe in God, they can rarely deeply define what they mean when they use the word *God*. When the Bible is used to define God, several conflicting definitions are available. Even fiery fundamentalist ministers who shout out, "The Bible says…" during their sermons can't help but describe God in a way that the Bible itself contradicts. This is one reason why debates about God tend to be highly emotional but are not particularly insightful.

Defining the word *God* is a little like defining the word *love*. Defining love requires establishing what kind of love someone is talking about. Love is one of those things that is difficult to prove intellectually, even though most people choose to believe in it at some level. One of the difficulties is that words are dualistic, and they don't do a great job of describing things that are non-dualistic.

Merriam-Webster takes a stab at defining God in these ways:

1. The supreme or ultimate reality: such as

   a: the Being perfect in power, wisdom, and goodness who is worshipped…as creator and ruler of the universe;
   b: the incorporeal divine Principle ruling over all as eternal Spirit: infinite Mind;

2. Being or object that is worshipped as having more than natural attributes and powers;
3. person or thing of supreme value;
4. powerful ruler.[2]

Webster gives us a lot to synthesize, which illuminates why it is easier for theists and atheists to use simple caricatures. For example, a being on a throne is easy for Christians to conceptualize and atheists to deny.

Defining God is not a new problem. There were various names for God long before Judaism began, and Moses was said to have declared God's name as the tetragrammaton, YHWH (*Yahweh*). Different strands of scripture have used different names for God. *Yahweh* is considered untranslatable but is a variant of the Hebrew "to be." It can be rendered in past, present, or future tense, viewed as "being" itself, or as the Ground of Being. YHWH was regarded as too sacred to be uttered and was replaced in synagogue rituals by the Hebrew word *Adonai* ("My Lord").

In Christian churches, God is defined through organizational dogma as well as artistic renditions. God is mostly portrayed as a bearded, gray-haired, European man. Beyond the physical characteristics churches use, more qualitatively, some churches portray God as

---

[2] *Merriam-Webster.com Dictionary*, s.v. "god," accessed September 28, 2021, https://www.merriam-webster. com/dictionary/god.

a God of love, while others embrace an angry God. The Bible can be used to support either of these definitions.

Angry God caricatures often win out because most churches have business models that benefit from positioning God the Father as an eternally judgmental being who controls everything and has entrusted day-to-day operations to local church leaders. Tithes and offerings are said to be signs of one's love for and commitment to God as a sovereign being, with the implication (if not outright teaching) that serious giving can result in serious blessings. With fundamentalist business models, the promise of mansions in heaven after death is used as a carrot and eternal torture in hell after death as the corresponding stick. Hell is also used as a recruiting tool, first to convince people to become Christians and then to encourage them to want to save everyone they care about by inviting them to church to avoid an eternity of torment. From a business model perspective, hell is a gift that keeps on giving.

CREATING GOD IN MAN'S IMAGE

Imagine visiting a classroom of toddlers in grammar school learning their ABC's and visiting them again a decade later in high school only to find that they were still going through the same curriculum. You would be shocked and perhaps saddened that they hadn't progressed beyond the mere basics. But isn't this situation essentially what happens in dogmatic Christian churches? Children learn about a simple God in Sunday school and then, for consistency's sake, are told to keep believing the same way when they are adults.

Some choose to deconstruct because they stop believing in the definition of God they were taught as children. When they ask questions about it, they are told to keep believing or maybe even that the devil is causing their doubts. The God deconstructing Christians stop believing in is typically the sovereign man-on-a-throne type. This suspension of belief can lead some to leave the faith entirely and redefine themselves as atheists or agnostics. During the transition, it's common for dogmatic Christians to trade in their previous fundamentalist beliefs about God for fundamentalist *non*-beliefs.

The common conceptual model of God the Father in Christianity is a man-like God joined via the Trinity to the Son and Holy Spirit. In modern language, this Godhead should technically have the pronouns they/them/their. But when described in churches and in the Bible, God is always a he/him/his. Further reinforcing church business models, God usually loves and hates the same things that the leader of the church does. While at some level, Christians can acknowledge that the nature of God is beyond their human capacity to fully comprehend, in practice, there is a strong attachment to the dualistic, sovereign, God-on-a-throne image that Christians are taught as kids.

Genesis 1:27 says that God created man in his own image. With a desire to connect the unfamiliar to the familiar, ancient texts are full of anthropomorphisms, or human-like images, for God and God's activities. Human language struggles to speak about the invisible and ineffable. When theology attempts to strip away all anthropomorphisms, God can become very abstract. This is not necessarily a bad practice, but the transition away from man-like imagery can be difficult for people who need concrete metaphors.

DECONSTRUCTING IN REAL LIFE: *"Growing up, I was heavily involved in the ministry and looked to the Bible for answers and therapy. I had a purity-culture marriage with a husband who was narcissistic and abusive, but the church didn't believe we should divorce, and they proactively protected him. I experienced many guilt trips, much gaslighting, and a lot of manipulative 'love.' I was kept off-balance by being told not to trust my thoughts. I had to deconstruct to get away and be able to embrace a non-abusive God."*

God is portrayed in man's image through Bible stories that depict God walking around the garden of Eden, interacting with Moses, writing the Ten Commandments with his own finger, and getting mad at the Israelites when they do not follow his advice. This caricature leads angry people to create a vengeful God, needy people to create a God who can help them get through a crisis, loving people to see a merciful God, and financially motivated people to see God as the source of their prosperity. When something good happens, they praise God for their good fortune, and when something bad happens, they lament over God's wrath or mysterious ways.

Objectifying God as an all-powerful being and believing that everything is part of his master plan doesn't hold true in life as we know it. Consider the story of Johnny Frank Garrett. Garrett was a 17-year-old boy convicted of raping and strangling a nun to death in a Catholic convent in 1982.

The point of this example is not to question how a sovereign God would have allowed such a tragedy to happen to a nun—to one of his own, in a place of his own. The point is that when the dualistic definition of a sovereign God does not hold up in real life, it is foolish to throw up one's hands and say that God works in mysterious ways. Either God is wrong, or the sovereign definition of God is wrong. When reality and dogma are at odds, less conscious people will often embrace dogma, and more conscious people will use their intuition and common sense.

This story is not over yet. Consider this excerpt from an interview with Garrett, who described memories of a childhood so horrific that he had to refer to himself in the third person.

"He was being fucked."
By who?
"His father."
Yeah, and who else?
"Other men that he met through him." "Boys." "A dog."
Why the dog and boys? Tell me about that. What was going on?
"We was being filmed."

Johnny Frank Garrett was a victim of child pornography, abused and pimped out by his own father. Either this was all part of a sovereign God's master plan, or the sovereign definition of God is wrong. Doesn't the fact that this sovereign depiction of God exists at all demonstrate how powerful the dualistic and dogmatic characterization in the Christian business model is?

Conceptualizing God micromanaging the events of people's lives, from losing a child to winning the lottery, serves church business models well. But things happen in life with no need for the supernatural. Some are in our control, some are in the control of others, and sometimes, random events occur due to incalculable and unpredictable sets of conditions and preconditions. Thus, the definition of God as a master controller does not fit with the realities of life.

A problem with using a dualistic and dogmatic definition of God is its inability to improve with better information and greater personal consciousness. Throughout history, dogmatic people have fought wars in the name of a man-like God against enemies who fought back in the name of the same God. Isn't this tragic? Conceptualizing God like a man in control of everything is easy for children to grasp but foolish for Christian adults to dogmatically protect.

IS THERE AN ALTERNATIVE TO THE MAN-LIKE GOD?

When reconsidering God while deconstructing, one option is to abandon the dualistic caricature and live as an atheist. Another is to suspend judgment and declare oneself an agnostic of some sort—on a spectrum somewhere between hopeful and unhopeful. A third option is to embrace God in a more spiritual way.

Can God be taken seriously without believing in the dualistic man in the sky? Many Christians and ex-Christians don't believe so. While ancient writers undoubtedly objectified God, deconstructing Christians can also make a biblical case for embracing God in other ways if they wish to. If someone chooses, God can be interpreted through verses like 2 Corinthians 3:17, where Paul writes, "Now the Lord is the Spirit, and where the Spirit of the Lord is, there is freedom." In John 4:24, Jesus said that God was "spirit, and his worshipers must worship in the spirit and in truth." In 1 John 4:16, the Bible also says, "God is love, and that whoever lives in love lives in God, and God in them." God as love can be further reflected upon through 1 Corinthians 13, where Paul beautifully writes about the nature of love, including the following attributes.

- Patience
- Forgiveness
- Trust
- Kindness
- Truthfulness
- Hope
- Humility
- Protection
- Perseverance

In the same passage, Paul writes that when he was a child, he talked like a child, thought like a child, and reasoned like a child. But when he became a man, he put the ways of childhood behind him. In Galatians 5, he writes that the fruits of the Spirit are "love, joy, peace, forbearance, kindness, goodness, faithfulness, gentleness and self-control, and that against such things there is no law" (vv. 22–23). Paul also writes in 1 Corinthians 3:16: "Don't you realize that all of you together are the temple of God and that the Spirit of God lives in you?"

Christians do not need to define God like a 5-year-old if they don't wish to. People can use the same Bible to embrace God more spiritually and contemplatively. Christians can embrace God as love and God as spirit and *I Am*-ness (i.e., Being). God can exist in each moment rather than as an objectified being on a throne, sitting somewhere above the clouds. In this way, God can be embraced in a richer, more spiritual way.

When thinking about God *as* love, *love* can be used as a noun and a verb. *God* is normally only used as a noun, but God as love, spirit, and *I Am*-ness can certainly be thought of in this way. Jesus essentially turned God into a verb when he prioritized love, connection, and service over dogmatic legalism. Jesus' life in the Bible was often contemplative. Christians today can experience God in this way as well—experiencing God in the grandest and smallest ways, like the beauty of a star-filled evening, the joy in a child's laugh, the smell of a rose, the warmth of a summer's sunrise, and the taste of an apple right off a tree.

God can be embraced spiritually as the great *I AM*. To do this, we need to be able to get out of our heads and open our hearts. For many, this conceptualization will be an improvement over objectifying God in ways that don't fit with reality, that encourage Christians to act like the Pharisees in the New Testament, and that suggest God is a cosmic puppeteer behind their fortunes and misfortunes.

*   *   *

Embracing God as the great *I AM* is like connecting to the nature of consciousness itself. While this is possible biblically, most churches have not built their business models around this version of God. As spirit, love, and the great *I AM,* God is the source of being, the Ground of Being, and being itself. In this sense, through God, we can reflect on questions such as why something exists rather than nothing? What is it that knits the universe together and gives it life? What is the source of life, breath, energy, and vitality? How is it that I feel connected not just to myself, but to other people, and other creatures, plants, stars, and to life itself? God can be used to explain our connection to being and its source by doing this.

> The Christian caricature of God is generally a man-like being who seems to love and hate the same things that the leader of the church does. Christians can think about God in a richer, more spiritual way by transcending the dualistic dogma they learned as children. Embracing God more spiritually as spirit, love, and the great I AM is a possible biblical choice, even though most churches do not build their business models on this version. As the great I AM, God is love and love is God, and can be shared in the same way that people share the same air.

Through *I AM*-ness, as when people's minds are calmed during meditation and their hearts are opened, profound questions can be answered in ways that are beyond our normal abilities to explain yet are existentially too important to ignore. Does this come from God? It depends upon how we define God.

While unprovable in a laboratory environment, one way to embrace God as the great *I AM* is like the way we think about consciousness. Consciousness is the silent voice and observer within each of us. It is both obvious and mysterious, the part of us that never ages, no matter how old we get, that we know we can trust unconditionally, and that we can recognize as being honestly and uniquely *us*.

Taking this a step further, conceptualizing God as universal consciousness is another unprovable but potentially helpful way to contemplate God as spirit, love, and the great *I AM*. Panpsychism conceptualizes the universe like a giant mind. Unlike a dualistic man on a throne, God can similarly be embraced with all the majesty of viewing the universe through the Hubble space telescope. In this sense, humans are literally made in God's image like the Bible says—composed of the same matter as the universe itself.

For more mystical Christians, God can be embraced without form, providing the space for everything that exists to exist, like the early *Yahweh* definition as "being" itself or the Ground of Being. There is so much that we don't know, so is it really that irrational to believe in something greater than ourselves? While the scientific method is powerful, and Christianity, Inc. could learn quite a bit from embracing it more fully, people can focus far too much on the individual notes of rationalism and miss out on the overall music of life.

When God is forced into a dualistic and dogmatic box, it diminishes God. The great *I AM* need not be compartmentalized, and "God" should not need to be used as a tool to manipulate others and generate revenue. A valid choice for deconstructing Christians is to embrace God as the great *I AM* with no boundaries in the same way that love has no boundaries. In this sense, God is love and love is God, and can be shared in the same way that we all share the same air.

GOD AS LOVE

Jesus as God's son prioritized love above all else throughout the gospels. In the eighth chapter of John, when Jesus protected the adulteress from her law-based death sentence, he asked for the first stone to be cast by someone who had not sinned. Jesus touched the untouchables and said that the kingdom of heaven is not here or there but within. During his Sermon on the Mount in Matthew 5, he encouraged people to live non-dualistic lives of love, forgiveness, and human connection:

- "You have heard that it was said, 'Love your neighbor and hate your enemy.' But I tell you, love your enemies and pray for those who persecute you, that you may be children of your Father in heaven."[3]
- God causes "the sun to rise on the evil and the good and sends rain on the righteous and the unrighteous."[4]
- "If you love those who love you, what reward will you get? Are not even the tax collectors doing that?"[5]
- "If you greet only your own people, what are you doing more than others? Do not even pagans do that?"[6]

By prioritizing love as most important, Jesus provided a compass for Christian deconstruction. When he was asked, "Teacher, which is the greatest commandment in the Law?" Jesus replied: "Love the Lord your God with all your heart and with all your soul and with all your mind. This is the first and greatest commandment. And the second is like it: 'Love your neighbor as yourself.'"[7]

Jesus also said, "Do not judge, or you too will be judged."[8] In Matthew 9:13, he said, "I desire mercy, not sacrifice." He told his disciples to engage in the world not through dogmatic beliefs but through compassionate actions.

When Jesus fought with the religious leaders of his day over their organizational corruption and dogmatic legalism, he accused them of not knowing the God they said they were serving. Jesus practiced religion as a verb instead of a noun, helping the sick and hungry and

---

[3] Vv. 43–45a, NIV

[4] V. 45b, NIV

[5] V. 46, NIV

[6] V. 47, NIV

[7] Matt. 22:36–40

[8] Matt. 7:1, NIV

living a life of worldly nonattachment. Jesus was consistently on the side of the sick, poor, and disenfranchised.

Throughout the gospels, Jesus went to where the pain was. He chose ordinary people to be his disciples and did not cater to the rich and powerful. He did not focus on sin but on the suffering caused by sin and was loving and compassionate to everyone other than the religiously pious. Jesus was consistently in the streets healing, feeding, loving, and forgiving others. He was not there for the righteous but for the broken.

Jesus did not try to start a new religion. Instead, he worked to improve the religion that was already in place, from law to love, an eye for an eye to turning the other cheek, judgment to non-judgment, and from being served to serving others. So, what might a Jesus-centric Christian practice look like today? This is the subject of the next chapter, connected to my own Christian deconstruction. I don't consider it *the* answer, but rather a thought-starter to try to help you create *your* answer.

CHAPTER SUMMARY IN STORYBOOK FORM

- Once upon a time, Christians described God in dualistic man-like terms.
- Every day, Christian leaders taught their congregations that God was up in heaven and people were down on earth.
- One day, Christians began to conceptualize God less dualistically and more like spirit, love, and the great I AM.
- Because of that, they embraced God in more spiritual ways.
- Because of that, Christians focused on loving people, not judging them, forgiving their enemies, and helping those in need.
- Until finally, Christianity became known as the religion of love.
- And then they were able to live happily ever after.

7

My Personal Deconstruction Journey

A new command I give you: Love one another. As I have loved you, so you must love one another. By this everyone will know that you are my disciples, if you love one another.

John 13:34–35

CHRISTIANS ARE SOMETIMES a little like 35-year-old friends on Facebook. Some are still reliving what happened in high school, while others are living their lives with great courage and enthusiasm. Deconstructing Christians are courageous, pursuing truth as they challenge their core dogmatic beliefs and the systems that have produced them. Deconstruction is a catalyst for spiritual transformation, like when Paul writes that those who belong to Christ become new: the old life is gone, and a new life begins.[1]

---

[1] See 2 Cor. 5:17, NLT translation, especially.

This chapter focuses on the "So what?" and "Now what?" of the previous chapters, as seen through the lens of my own Christian deconstruction. I do not suggest in any way that my personal journey will be the best path for you. But it may provide some thought starters for Christians just beginning the process or for those who wish to take their thinking to another level.

For some Christians, especially those who have been traumatized, staying a Christian in any form may not be a viable option, at least for the foreseeable future. But thanks to an expanding community and a growing number of social media and counseling resources, deconstructing Christians do not need to go it alone. At the same time, the process is a very personal thing, and everyone's deconstruction is unique. It does not happen *to* people as much as it happens *through* them, often one day and personal experience at a time.

For me, deconstruction was transformative. It helped me become more spiritual, rational, *and* conscious as a Christian. I was able to find a Christian faith that I could honestly and enthusiastically believe in: one where I could dance to the music of life in an ever-changing world with beliefs that were personally adaptable, yet spiritually unshakable.

* * *

To use *Christian Snapshot* language that will be further explained in Chapter 9, my personal deconstruction resulted in a shift from the supernatural and literalistic belief system I was taught as a child to one that is much more contemplative and humanistic. While everyone's path is different, this chapter describes my personal journey over many years. (See Figure 7.1, "My Personal Christian Deconstruction Journey.")

While these steps did not happen in the completely linear way that the figure might imply, they are true directionally. Even today, I sometimes move forward and backward, within and across them. As I look back, I can see that I often didn't realize these were the steps I was taking until afterwards. There may be future changes as well, and there might even be additional steps I take from here.

I will only know after I get there.

Figure 7.1. My Personal Christian Deconstruction Journey

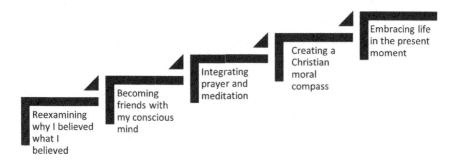

STEP ONE: REEXAMINING WHY I BELIEVED WHAT I BELIEVED

Due to the five interdependences described in the earlier chapters, the Christian belief system I had was difficult to deconstruct. My first step was to honestly challenge what I believed by assessing to what degree my beliefs could be validated by outsiders. If a personal belief could not be independently validated by non-Christians, I allowed myself to accept that it might not be literally true. At the same time, I felt free to honor everything I had believed before, but in a more spiritual way, like with the intent behind Jesus' parables. Reviewing Christian dogma this way produced a liberating, yet loving shift in my perspective over many years.

I was able to transcend my literalistic childhood beliefs at my own pace and in my own way, which helped me grow without being rushed. These changes didn't destroy my love for Christianity any more than medical doctors lose their love for medicine as they evolve in their knowledge and practices. Through my progression, I was able to embrace my Christian past without being imprisoned by its belief systems.

As I became more conscious, I was able to free myself from the arthritic nature of the dogma I had been taught growing up. It seems like this is what Jesus was doing when he debated the religious leaders of his day. One of the Pharisees' problems was that they were unable to grow spiritually because they could not break free from their legalistic beliefs. Jesus said, "These people honor me with their lips, but their hearts are far from me. They worship me in vain; their teachings are merely human rules."[2]

The Pharisees used scriptures to condemn others, while Jesus used the same scriptures to tell a different story. In Jesus' telling, love fulfilled the law, non-judgment was a spiritual practice, continuous forgiveness was expected, and there was a moral obligation to help people who were sick and hungry.

During my first step, I spent time deeply reflecting on some of the unconscious Christian practices that I had observed throughout my life. In so doing, I deliberately thought about areas where I had seen certain Christian churches and church leaders go astray. For example, I witnessed:

- The use of Bible verses to justify hatred, even though Jesus said that love was the greatest commandment
- Disregard for Jesus' guidance to "give to Caesar what is Caesar's" and the creation of a political Christianity
- The embracing of leaders who solicit money and who promise that God will pay them back later or after they die
- Using the Bible to justify and sustain corrupt organizational business models
- The fight against and denial of modern scientific evidence based on what Moses wrote more than three millennia ago
- Claims to authority to speak on behalf of a parochially-defined God through "words of knowledge"
- Insistence that dogma cannot be challenged for supernatural reasons
- The promise of miracles to collect donations from the vulnerable and terminally ill.

I eventually concluded that complicated supernatural answers were not necessary when simple natural ones could explain things just as well or better. For example, the Bible did not require supernatural

---

[2]Matthew 15:8–9, NIV

intervention from the Holy Spirit in order for it to be created. Its existence can be explained simply and naturally. Beginning thousands of years ago, scribes wrote a collection of disparate documents that the Catholic Church eventually compiled into the Christian Bible. Protestants later used parts of it as their foundation. While the Bible is a wonderful human achievement and important to the Christian faith, it can be both things without needing to have been supernaturally created.

Within the Bible itself, I also concluded that supernaturalism did not need to be believed literally. For example, my Christian faith did not and does not need to depend upon believing that the Red Sea was literally parted or that Jesus literally calmed the Sea of Galilee. I am free to believe these things at some level if I wish, but I discovered I can just as easily say, "I don't know, and it doesn't really matter to what's most important in my Christian practice."

Being intellectually honest did not water down the Bible for me. If anything, it made it more meaningful and credible. Without dogma, I was able to read the Bible without any doubts and enthusiastically embrace it as a treasured history of early Judaism and Christianity. I learned to appreciate that today's Christians and Jews have overcome many bad practices, including slavery, xenophobia, misogyny, homophobia, and other human rights tragedies that included killing rebellious children. I also came to believe that for churches to choose to use the Bible legalistically to cause human trauma today is a horrible choice and inconsistent with what Jesus prioritized as most important. There are many examples of bad human behavior in the Bible. But those examples do not give anyone permission to use the Bronze Age-based history of the faith to hurt others in the name of Christ. For example, harming non-heterosexuals, people of color, women, or non-cisgender people in any way can hardly be justified as "Christian."

During this step of my journey, it became clear to me that if Christianity could not transcend many of its ancient dogmatic beliefs, accelerated declines were highly likely. Rather than abandon Christian dogma entirely, I simply changed my relationship to it. The unprovable was not required for me to focus on what Jesus prioritized as most important: greater love, connection, and service.

STEP TWO: BECOMING FRIENDS WITH MY CONSCIOUS MIND

One of the most life-changing parts of my deconstruction was learning to better understand the nature of my mind. During this stage, I learned that I was not my thoughts and that when I was not mentally conscious, my thoughts were often not my friends. In this step, I benefitted greatly from meditation and silent prayer (Step Three).

During my second step, I learned to watch my thoughts come and go. I could increasingly see that many of my long-held assumptions were simply thoughts. As explained in Chapter 2, I saw that Christianity was not dualistically black and white, but that it has many shades of gray, and that replacing inflexible dogma with direct experience is essential to knowing the truth. I saw how dualism had been pounded into me from birth. Like everyone else, from the time I took my first breath, I was given a name and birth certificate and dualistically separated from everyone else on earth. I was thrust into a social structure where I was taught to believe certain things, compare myself to others, and accept that my thoughts and I were the same things.

I saw that for my whole life I had been engaged in unconscious thinking without realizing it. My unconscious mind had been like a horse without a saddle or bridle. Without those, most of the advantages favor the horse. I discovered that my unconscious mind had pulled me into a world of thought without my knowledge or permission. It had been fooled into believing that I was the egoic picture I had painted for myself, an ego that often made me miserable by continually wanting things to be different than they were.

Without my realizing it, compulsive and obsessive thinking had caused me to ignore many of the most precious moments of my life. With greater consciousness, I have been able to live more abundantly. I am able to understand the difference between being engaged in my life and being lost in my thoughts.

During this stage, I positively embraced how I would eventually lose everything I ever accumulated or achieved. Since I knew how the movie was going to end, why not live less obsessively? The idea of "treasures in heaven" became anathema. As a result, I experienced equanimity for the first time in my life, which produced an enormous psychological relief. I was finally able to get off the merry-go-round of my compulsive thoughts and see more clearly how easy it was to achieve success yet still have a miserable life.

Prior to this part of my deconstruction, my mind had been like a Whack-A-Mole game. Thoughts randomly popped up for no apparent rhyme nor reason. My unconscious mind loved to solve problems, and if there were no problems to solve, it had little trouble making up new ones. It thrived on separation, comparison, conflict, and enemies. My epiphany during this step was the realization that by pursuing happiness, I had made it impossible to be happy. As soon I had achieved one goal, I was on to the next one.

The futility of repetitive thinking became more apparent during this step. I could increasingly see how often I repeated the same thoughts in my head, as if repetition would make a difference. It was like being in a car with someone who keeps saying the very same thing over and over during a long trip. My repetitive thoughts were often fixated on negative and anxiety-producing things like worries and regrets, and narcissistic things like living up to self-imposed expectations. All this worry and egoic thinking didn't change a thing; it only kept me from engaging with my direct experience.

As I became more friendly with my conscious mind, I was increasingly able to poke fun at my unconscious tendencies. By labeling them with humor, I took away some of their power. It was a little like being at a dinner table with three guests. One guest was always quietly observing what was going on. This guest was like the stillness of my consciousness. The second guest was focused on getting important work done. This guest was like my problem-solving brain. The third guest was like the obnoxious guy who tries to dominate the conversation and eat all the food. This guest was like the nature of my unconscious mind—generating thoughts whether I wanted them or not, dwelling repetitively on the past and future, always trying to look good to others, and usually wanting things to be different than they were.

Figure 7.2. Characteristics of the Unconscious Mind

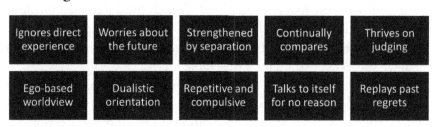

Ignores direct experience	Worries about the future	Strengthened by separation	Continually compares	Thrives on judging
Ego-based worldview	Dualistic orientation	Repetitive and compulsive	Talks to itself for no reason	Replays past regrets

My mind had tricked me into believing that I was the story I had created for myself and that others had created for me. During this stage, I realized that I was neither my thoughts nor these stories. I also discovered that the conceptual world was not an accurate world, the past was an imperfect memory, and the future was an imperfect forecast. With greater awareness I was able to get out of my head, further engage in my direct experience, and trust in the emergence of my life.

The interplay between my conscious and unconscious mind was and is a little like an American baseball game. The unconscious mind throws a lot of pitches, but with greater consciousness, I can increase my ability to watch the bad ones go by without swinging. With greater consciousness, I can relate to my thoughts in a healthier way. While I can't control what my next thought will be, I can control what I do with it.

When Jesus went on his 40-day retreat in the wilderness, the Bible describes his dialog with the devil through the lens of consciousness.[3] When the devil suggests physical comfort, Jesus does not swing at that pitch. He says that comfort is not everything and stays in the moment. The devil then pitches greater personal power, and Jesus again does not swing. The devil then pitches for Jesus to demonstrate his power, and Jesus again does not swing and stays in the moment. This describes the nature of the mind. It wants things—like Jesus' temptations—to be different than they are. It strives for greater comfort, power, and status. But, like Jesus, the conscious mind has the capability to let these pitches go by and be more fully engaged in the present moment.

During this step of my deconstruction, I became better at managing the commentator in my head, become more conscious as a person, and

---

[3]See Luke 4

was able to live a more spiritual life in each moment. I still had personal goals but became more equanimous when pursuing them. I learned how to say *yes* to what is, and I experienced greater peace as a result.

STEP THREE: INTEGRATING PRAYER AND MEDITATION

I was taught to pray out loud as a child, even through rhymes: "Now I lay me down to sleep; I pray the Lord my soul to keep." Soon, I learned to bargain for things that I wanted from an objectified God on a throne in heaven. Meditation was not a significant part of the Christian landscape during my formative years. There was some awareness of mystics like Francis of Assisi and Thomas Merton, but both were outside of the Christian mainstream. Meditation for the most part was considered in the realm of Buddhists.

Mindfulness meditation became an increasingly important part of my Christian practice during this phase of my deconstruction. I imagine that Jesus' 40-day prayer retreats included a good bit of contemplation. In the sixth chapter of Matthew, Jesus told his followers to pray meditatively instead of out loud:

> And when you pray, do not be like the hypocrites, for they love to pray standing in the synagogues and on the street corners to be seen by others. Truly I tell you, they have received their reward in full. But when you pray, go into your room, close the door, and pray to your Father, who is unseen. Then your Father, who sees what is done in secret, will reward you. And when you pray, do not keep on babbling like pagans, for they think they will be heard because of their many words. Do not be like them, for your Father knows what you need before you ask him.[4]

Jesus' disciples had to directly ask him how to pray and this further supported my use of meditation and silent prayer. When asked, Jesus told his disciples to pray in what we now know as the

---

[4]Matt. 6:5–8, NIV

Lord's Prayer with reverence, commitment, contentment, forgiveness, and humility.[5]

I had seen how spoken prayer had been misused by religious leaders to control and extort money from their flocks. It was also used to encourage individuals, me included, to cultivate the unconscious mind's desire to always want things to be different than they are. Meditation seemed to be much closer to true prayer.

The continuum of consciousness regarding prayer seemed to run the gamut from memorized, recited children's prayers to extemporaneous prayers of negotiation, appreciative spiritual prayers, and meditative prayer, where language was eliminated altogether. Meditative prayer helped me to pray more consciously, be more engaged in the present moment, and embrace life's preciousness instead of perpetually wanting things to be different.

As a daily practice, meditation and silent prayer helped me to see and detach from my unconscious thought patterns (at least for brief periods). My own contemplative journey during this step evolved from "I think, therefore I am," to "I think too much, which is keeping me from being who I am," to "By transcending thought, I can be more connected to the great *I AM*." Deconstructing prayer in this way made a major difference in my life.

For non-meditators, learning to meditate has never been easier. There are many good books, videos, and apps readily available. Deconstructing Christians do not need to reinvent the wheel and can begin with out-of-the-box mindfulness meditation courses. Then, as their minds begin to calm down, meaningful Christian beliefs can be incorporated. Some possibilities are included later in this chapter. Meditation provides many benefits. It is an area where science has caught up with religion, helping millions of Christians and non-Christians alike experience better mental, emotional, spiritual, and physical health.

Meditative prayer helped me to loosen the tight grip that my ego had on my life's steering wheel and instead enjoy the view from the passenger seat. Then and now, my mind is perpetually transformed through meditation. Through meditation, my mind has evolved from

---

[5]See Luke 11

an anxiety-ridden raging river to a much calmer body of water. My happiness does not depend as much on everything going right, but on my ability to become right with everything that is going on.

Table 7.1 may help to provide further context for understanding some of the differences between traditional and meditative prayer.

Table 7.1. Traditional vs. Meditative Prayer

TRADITIONAL PRAYER	MEDITATIVE PRAYER
Has an agenda	Is still and observational
Speaks or thinks actively through words	Sits and listens
Focuses on the future or past	Engages in the present moment
Speaks for an inside group	Strives for connection
Conforms to dogma	Engages in a process of discovery
Prayer has a goal	Prayer is the goal
Based on thought	Transcends thought
Dualistic and ego-based	Non-dualistic and selfless
We are our thoughts and beliefs	Thoughts and beliefs are like vapors
Has a direction	Is the direction
Strives for more	Loosens from attachments
Lost in discursive thoughts	Aware of discursive thoughts
Prayer is an event	Prayer is continuous
Like a clenched fist	Like an open palm
Serious	Playful
The mind is like a raging river	The mind is like a calm pond

TRADITIONAL PRAYER	MEDITATIVE PRAYER
The purpose is to become	The purpose is to be
Pious	Humble
Negotiates in God's name	Appreciates in God's name
Tries to feel righteous	Tries to simply feel
Views sin as a supernatural battle	Views sin as a personal practice area
Asks for something from God	Lets go and lets God

Jesus suggested that his followers live in the moment like the lilies. Meditative prayer can help Christians achieve this. With greater consciousness, we can watch our thoughts come and go and engage in our direct experience in a more concentrated way. Personal equanimity can increase as these capabilities strengthen. This connection to the present moment is like the state of *I AM* in the Old and New Testaments. The present moment is the one constant force in our lives, and with each new breath, we are given the opportunity to experience rebirth.

*   *   *

DECONSTRUCTING IN REAL LIFE: *"In my church, there was the expectation to be perfect as Christ was perfect. It was disingenuous, there was a double standard, and it became exhausting. Purity culture and not affirming those in the LGBTQ community was finally too much to digest. I can't defend a faith that causes such psychological harm. As I deconstructed, I found that my church friends and even family relationships turned out to be conditional."*

During the third step of my deconstruction, I began to understand sin very differently from what I had been taught as a child. I could see original sin as a dogmatic remnant and a poor way to explain how the unconscious mind worked. Listening to arguments about original sin became increasingly fascinating. To recognize that humans had evil thoughts did not require, nor could these thoughts be improved by, believing that sin was the result of a 6,000-year-old supernatural curse caused by Adam eating a piece of fruit in the Garden of Eden.

It became clear that I did not need to see sin as a supernatural battle between demons and angels like I had been taught as a kid. Yet it *could* be a good practice area for addressing, in Jesus' language, the beams in my own eyes. Through meditation, these beams became better understood and were more compassionately labeled. Through this combination, they were denied some of their power. Everyone has unconscious thoughts, but we are not those thoughts. By lovingly labeling the beams in our eyes, and not swinging at the pitches, we can watch their grips loosen, and in some cases, fade away entirely. This is obviously not the case with mental illness, where professional help is essential.

With meditation, I have been better able to become at one with the music of my direct experience. Life has become more of a dance in the moment and less of a march into the future. If consciousness could be defined in a single word, for me that word would be *now*. In two words, *I AM*. Now is the only place where life and the peace that passes understanding can exist. Spirituality is not supernatural. It is super-natural.

Over time, I was able to make the shift from saying prayers to becoming prayer. When I get anxious, I can step back, take some deep breaths, fully engage in the moment, and then patiently watch my mind's mental chatter come and go. Prayer went from being a discrete event with an agenda and wish list to a continuous way of living in and appreciating life in the present moment.

Meditative prayer led to a profound personal shift in my life. Instead of constantly wanting things to be different, I appreciate life as it is, right here, right now. To illustrate the difference, Table 7.2, "Psalm 23 via Conscious vs. Unconscious Orientations," interprets the 23rd Psalm through both lenses.

Table 7.2. Psalm 23 via Conscious vs. Unconscious Orientations

23rd Psalm (KJV)	Conscious Equanimity	Unconscious Striving
The LORD is my shepherd; I shall not want.	Compulsive wanting is not needed.	God will give me what I want in the future.
He maketh me to lie down in green pastures: he leadeth me beside the still waters.	Equanimity is my natural spiritual state.	God will give me good stuff if he likes me.
He restoreth my soul: he leadeth me in the paths of righteousness for his name's sake.	Restoration comes with each new breath in each moment.	The current state is never good enough.
Yea, though I walk through the valley of the shadow of death, I will fear no evil: for thou art with me; thy rod and thy staff they comfort me.	Embrace life as it is in each moment with comfort and without fear.	We are all going to die and should strive for God's comfort when it happens.
Thou preparest a table before me in the presence of mine enemies: thou anointest my head with oil; my cup runneth over.	I have enough.	I am entitled to get a lot.
Surely goodness and mercy shall follow me all the days of my life: and I will dwell in the house of the LORD for ever.	The house of the LORD is within, eternally now, all the days of my life.	I will go to the house of the LORD after I die.

* * *

Paul's description of the peace that transcends understanding and that guards hearts and minds (Phil. 4:7) is a good description of the equanimity that comes from meditative prayer. Like a clear pond once the mud has settled after a heavy rain, letting go and letting God can help to conceptualize and cultivate this peace that transcends understanding.

In good times, we can be grateful instead of prideful. In bad times, we can be accepting instead of resentful. With meditation and silent prayer as a continuous practice, I found that happiness was what happened when I stopped searching for it. In this sense, meditative prayer has helped me to cultivate several things:

- Having intentions without clinging to outcomes;
- Not trying to negotiate with God;
- Living in the present moment;
- Not needing an answer for everything;
- Discovering that the spiritual path leads within.

Meditation and silent prayer helped me become more equanimous during my deconstruction. If you think it could help you during your journey, a few Bible verses associated with Jesus' top priorities that might be useful for personal reflection are listed in Table 7.3, "Love, Connect, and Serve."

STEP FOUR: CREATING A CHRISTIAN MORAL COMPASS

A common trigger for deconstruction is when Christians act in non-Jesus-like ways, like how the Pharisees acted in the New Testament. Trapped by their own dogma and dogmatic business models, where Jesus stood for love, these Christians will sometimes act in subtle and even obviously hateful ways. Where he said to "judge not," they can be hyper-judgmental. Where Jesus said to give unto Caesar what was Caesar's, they have become essential gears in the U.S. political machine. Where Jesus fed the hungry and healed the sick, they have cried out against using taxes to redistribute wealth to the poor while simultaneously demanding tax-exempt status for their own churches.

113

Table 7.3. Love, Connect, and Serve[6]

LOVE: Loving God as spirit, our neighbors as ourselves, and ourselves in the image of God's love and as the great I Am
• Dear friends, let us love one another, for love comes from God. Everyone who loves has been born of God and knows God. Whoever does not love does not know God, because God is love. *1 John 4:7–8* • My command is this: Love each other as I have loved you. *John 15:12* • Show me your ways, O LORD, teach me your paths. *Psalm 25:4* • Be still and know that I am God. *Psalm 46:10* • Sing to the LORD a new song, sing to the LORD, all the earth. *Psalm 96:1* • This is the day the Lord has made; let us rejoice and be glad in it. *Psalm 118:24* • But the fruit of the Spirit is love, joy, peace, kindness, goodness, faithfulness, gentleness, and self-control. *Galatians 5:22–23*
CONNECT: Non-judgmental human connection with others
• How good and pleasant it is when brothers live together in unity! *Psalm 133:1* • May the God who gives endurance and encouragement give you a spirit of unity among yourselves as you follow Christ Jesus. *Romans 15:5* • Accept one another, then, just as Christ accepted you, in order to bring praise to God. *Romans 15:7* • Make my joy complete by being like-minded, having the same love, being one in spirit and purpose. *Philippians 2:2* • Do not be anxious about anything. And the peace of God will guard your hearts and your minds in Christ Jesus. *Philippians 4:6–7* • My purpose is that they may be encouraged in heart and united in love. *Colossians 2:2* • Make every effort to add to your faith goodness, knowledge, self-control, perseverance, godliness, kindness, and love. *2 Peter 5–8*

---

[6]All verses quoted in Table 7.2 are NIV.

SERVE: Help others as a Christian spiritual practice
• Blessed is the one who is kind to the needy. *Proverbs 14:21*
• Speak up for those who cannot speak for themselves, for the rights of all who are destitute. *Proverbs 31:8*
• Whatever you did for one of the least of these brothers of mine, you did it for me. *Matthew 25:40*
• Anyone who has two shirts should share with the one who has none, and anyone who has food should do the same. *Luke 3:11*
• Make a tree good and its fruit will be good or make a tree bad and its fruit will be bad, for a tree is recognized by its fruit. *Matthew 12:33*
• Carry each other's burdens, and in this way, you will fulfill the law of Christ. *Galatians 6:2*
• If anyone has material possessions and sees his brother in need but has no pity on him, how can the love of God be in him? *1 John 3:17*

During the fourth step of my deconstruction process, I tried to sort through all of this and determine what it truly meant to act like a Christian. To do this, I reflected on Christian ethics and morality through the lens of Jesus' priorities: love, connection, and service. After all, love was Jesus' greatest commandment, connection is a function of non-judgment and forgiveness, and service is directly related to Jesus' regular efforts to feed the hungry and heal the sick.

Love, connection, and service emerged as a Christian compass to replace the political action that has become the modern substitute for Christian ethics and morality. This was important to me because the current Christian system seems to be taking well-meaning Jesus followers and systematically turning them into radicalized Pharisees. I began to use the Christian love-connect-serve compass to think through a variety of questions, decisions, and situations through a conscious Christian lens.

The simple love-connect-serve compass seemed to make it easier to transcend non-Christ-like Christian ideas and practices. It was not constrained by dogmatic legalism and could be validated through direct experience. With love, connection, and service as the compass, some of the Bible's more Jesus-like principles seemed to come alive.

Principles like kindness, non-judgment, forgiveness, connection, wisdom, and making good Christian choices emerged with greater clarity. For example, very different from what I was seeing on social media and cable television, I was able to concentrate my Christian practice on things like the following:

1. Kindness:
   By practicing repaying evil with good and hate with compassion, I can watch what happens to the other person and to my own life.

2. Non-judgment:
   I can identify an area where I can stop judging myself and others. By being more loving, I can see if what I previously judged begins to improve on its own.

3. Forgiveness:
   Take time to reflect on a strained relationship and the role I personally played. By asking for forgiveness for my role, no matter how small, see if the tension softens.

4. Connection:
   I can help an enemy or adversary in an area where we share a common interest and see if the relationship improves.

5. Wisdom:
   Try to differentiate between dualistic judging and non-dualistic discerning. See if this makes me wiser and more loving.

6. Choices:
   When it is time to make an important choice, consider which alternative is more loving, connected, and helpful. See if this leads to better answers and greater equanimity.

In Christian and atheist debates, Christian leaders often suggest that morality requires religion. Yet while many Christians are moral people, morality is different than religiosity, and many Christians do and have done immoral things in the name of God, directly supported (or at least seemingly justified) by Bible verses.

DECONSTRUCTING IN REAL LIFE: *"Deconstruction was hard but freeing. I had outgrown my container and deconstructing helped me to become more understanding and empathetic. It was liberating but painful to think about the wasted years prior to my deconstruction. But for me, deconstructing was a survival mechanism. I still have anger and heartache for the deception, but I believe God is proud of me for having the courage to personally own my beliefs."*

By creating a Christian moral compass, I asked: when faced with an ethical question, what if I simply choose love over hate, connection over separation, and service over selfishness? While this approach will no doubt seem overly simplistic to many readers, Table 7.4, "Ethical Choices," shows the framework that emerged.

Table. 7.4. Ethical Choices

LESS CHRISTIAN MORALITY	←ETHICAL CHOICES→	MORE CHRISTIAN MORALITY
Hate – act to harm others	1. An action toward love is more moral and toward hate is less moral	**Love** – act with kindness to others
Judgment – look down on others in a dualistic way	2. An action toward connection is more moral and toward judgmental disconnection is less moral	**Connection** – reach out to others in a non-dualistic way
Selfishness – act to enhance personal privilege at the expense of the disenfranchised	3. A choice toward service is more moral and toward selfishness is less moral	**Service** – act to help those in need, including those we know and do not know personally

While this compass is not theologically complex, complicated legalism seems to have consistently led to Christians missing the forest for the trees when more Jesus-centric choices have conflicted with established church business models. Below is an example of how to relate the love-connect-serve compass to Jesus' Beatitudes in the Sermon of the Mount (See Table 7.5, "Jesus' Beatitudes and Christian Compass").

Table 7.5. Jesus' Beatitudes and Christian Compass

JESUS' BEATITUDES	CHRISTIAN COMPASS
Be the salt of the earth	Serve those in need
Be the light of the world	Serve those in need
Fulfill the law	Love others and yourself
Do not kill or be angry with others	Connect with others
Watch the mind	Love others and yourself
Forgive others continually	Love others and yourself
Love your enemies	Love others and yourself
Help those in need	Serve those in need
Your treasure is where your heart is	Serve those in need
Do not worry	Love others and yourself
Do not judge	Connect with others
Treat others as you want to be treated	Connect with others
People are recognized by their fruit	Serve those in need
Blessed are the poor in spirit	Serve those in need
Blessed are the meek	Connect with others
Blessed are the merciful	Love others and yourself
Blessed are the pure in heart	Connect with others

JESUS' BEATITUDES	CHRISTIAN COMPASS
Blessed are the peacemakers	Love others and yourself
Blessed are the righteous	Serve those in need
All of this builds your house on the rock	Love, Connect, and Serve

In my own practice, I found that using the love-connect-serve moral compass resulted in Christian decisions that were more Jesus-centric than many Christians were suggesting. Even today it seems to consistently produce better answers than those generated by complex adherence to dogmatic legalism. I hope others find this compass a viable tool to help them navigate the moral and ethical vagaries of daily Christian life—particularly in areas concerning personal conduct, human rights, and social policies.

STEP FIVE: EMBRACING LIFE IN THE PRESENT MOMENT

In John 10:10, Jesus said he came so that people could live more abundant lives. My personal ability to live more abundantly improved significantly during the fifth step of my deconstruction.

Living in the present moment and embracing Christianity without literalized dogma made my Christian practice come alive. As a more conscious Christian, I found that the core principles of the Christian faith were not in the dogma. They were living underneath it. It was like searching for my glasses and discovering that I was already wearing them.

By integrating what I learned in the first four steps, I was finally able to live my life abundantly right here, right now. Beginning with honestly questioning my beliefs, I became friends with my conscious mind, integrated prayer and meditation, created a simple Christian moral compass, and could finally begin to integrate it all into my daily Christian life. Without going through the mental gymnastics required by legalistic dogma, I was able to live abundantly in the here and now.

My Christianity no longer depended upon what someone else wanted me to believe. All I needed to do was choose love over hate, connection over separation, and service over selfishness. My Christianity became more like Jesus *and* became much more fun to practice.

> With greater consciousness, my Christian practice transcended dogmatic thinking and I was able to live a more abundant life. Beginning with questioning my beliefs, I became friends with my conscious mind, integrated prayer and meditation, created a simple Christian moral compass, and focused on living life in the present moment.

Through my deconstruction, I was able to free myself from dogma and focus directly on the core principles of the Christian faith. This was not secularism dressed up like religion. It was a more Jesus-centric way to practice the faith, relax in the midst of life's uncertainties, and trust in life as Jesus described: "Look at the birds of the air; they do not sow or reap or store away in barns, and yet your heavenly Father feeds them. Are you not much more valuable than they?"[7]

Christianity became a way to cultivate spiritual growth with an honest appreciation for accepting that there is much that we do not know, will never know, and don't need to pretend that we know. This has resulted in greater Christian consciousness as highlighted in Table 7.6, "Being a Conscious Christian."

If we keep doing what we have been doing, we will keep getting the results we have been getting. Challenging Christianity is not heresy, and people who are deconstructing are in good company. Jesus himself was accused of blasphemy when he tried to deconstruct the Jewish law into a religion of love. At the same time, deconstruction will inevitably result in conflicts because religious leaders are paid to fight when their business models get threatened.

Deconstruction did not destroy my Christian faith. It saved it by making it more meaningful. I can now read the Bible in a healthy way, as a historic Christian treasure rather than an unprovable literal history and prophetic prediction. Rejecting literalistic dogma has not

---

[7] Matt. 6:26, NIV

watered down my Christian faith. Rather, it has produced a Christian experience that is more honest, joyful, and equanimous. It is a mix of old and new, like music created when composers simultaneously respect yet transcend traditional musical conventions.

Table 7.6. Being a Conscious Christian

Being a conscious Christian is not...	Being a conscious Christian is...
About searching for something we don't have	About exploring what we already have
Being obsessed with finding the one right answer	Understanding that answers often emerge
Trying to get to the future	Being completely in this moment
Trying to create certainty	Embracing uncertainty
Wishing for a changed world	Seeing the world in a changed way
Fighting sin as a supernatural battle	Lovingly leaning into sin to learn from and transcend it
An out-of-body experience	An inner-body journey

During my deconstruction, I stopped *searching* for the answer and started *emerging* as the answer. This process ended up leading me to another question, which was whether it might be possible for congregations to deconstruct instead of experience further declines. Can a more conscious generation of Christian churches emerge? Could these organizations help people improve their lives and change the world for the better? If so, how might this work?

With these questions in mind, whereas this chapter has synthesized my personal deconstruction experience as an example for others, the next chapter is written through the perspective I have as a business transformation consultant about the Christian system more generally.

CHAPTER SUMMARY IN STORYBOOK FORM

- Once upon a time, people thought their churches decided whether they were Christians or not.
- Every day, people were given beliefs by their religious leaders and judged against the standards that their churches imposed.
- One day, Christians discovered that Christianity did not happen to them, but through them.
- Because of that, they replaced religious legalism with spiritual principles.
- Because of that, they became more conscious and focused on Jesus' priorities of love, connection, and service.
- Until finally, Christians were able to live more abundantly in the present moment.
- And then they were able to live happily ever after.

8

Rethinking Church

And let us consider how we may spur one another on toward love and good deeds, not giving up meeting together, as some are in the habit of doing, but encouraging one another.

Hebrews 10:24–25

I SPENT A significant amount of time with Bob Buford, author of the bestselling book *Halftime,* during the last five years of his life.[1] Along with management thinker Peter Drucker, Bob was one of the early business architects of the Evangelical megachurch. He and I were both on the board of the Drucker Institute, and I visited Bob often in Dallas. During my first conversation with Bob in Claremont, California, I asked for his opinion about a specific and well-known church. He predicted (correctly) that it would implode. He quoted Jim Collins' five stages of decline: (1) Hubris born of success; (2)

---

[1]Bob Buford, *Halftime: Moving from Success to Significance* (Grand Rapids, MI: Zondervan, 1994).

Undisciplined pursuit of more; (3) Denial of risk and peril; (4) Grasping for salvation; and (5) Capitulation to irrelevance or death.[2]

Declining churches today can learn a lot from declining non-Christian organizations. First, declining companies are almost always internally focused and perceive themselves to be doing fine at the point when they've reached the third stage of their decline, denial. Then, off the cliff they head. When they are founded, successful organizations focus on the market and offer something new and exciting. Then they begin to believe they are super smart, and in the case of Christian organizations, there is the further complication of believing they are blessed by God. Organizational leaders are often tempted to double down on their old business models, even when the market is telling them they need to change. Leaders of declining organizations commonly blame outsiders for their problems and deny that they are the ones doing something wrong. The declines accelerate and then the organizations become irrelevant, get taken over by someone else, or go out of business entirely.

This seems to be the story of the 21st-century Christian church. Younger members are deconstructing and leaving, these members are wrongly considered the problem, the leaders are doubling down on their one true way and scratching their heads as the declines continue. For decades, Christian churches have been losing their young people. This does not bode well for the future. They seem to be increasingly heading toward Collins' stage three, denial, as they continue to defend their dogmatic business models. If this can't be fixed, Collins' stage four, grasping for salvation, will turn some churches into Christian museums and others into empty lots.

Christian churches will require organizational transformation in the future. The Christian business models that are currently in place and the people paid to perpetuate them seem to only have two options. The first possibility is that growing numbers of young people will leave or never sign up to begin with, leading struggling churches with high overheads to become financially insolvent. The second possibility is for churches to congregationally deconstruct and then reinvent

---

[2]See Jim Collins' "Five Stages of Decline," available https://www.jimcollins.com/concepts/five-stages-of-decline.html. The concept can be studied more in depth in Collins' self-published *How the Mighty Fall* (2009).

themselves. It will be difficult if not impossible for denominations to do this top-down because the interdependencies outlined earlier in this book have been designed to prevent it. But it could happen one congregation at a time, led by small groups of deconstructing Christians with Jesus-centric faiths.

This chapter provides some thought starters for congregations that wish to deconstruct. It will not be easy because organizational transformation is complex: it requires changing how congregations, leaders, processes, and systems work and work together. It will take more than an ability to point out what's wrong; it will require groups of people working hand-in-hand to build upon what's still working to cocreate better futures together.

One thing that churches have going for them is the size and maturity of their asset-base. But, even if deconstruction happens one church at a time, there will be tensions between the need for change balanced with the need for continuity, as management thinker Peter Drucker (mentor to both Jim Collins and Bob Buford) pointed out. Continuity is needed to leverage existing assets, and change is required to redeploy them in a new way for a new age.

One way to think about congregational transformation is to first consider what a church without literalistic dogma—to the degree that this is addressed—might look like. For instance, in a Jesus-centric way, how can the church of the future best help people grow spiritually? How can it help people who are suffering, while also being intellectually honest and economically sustainable?

Can you imagine what a church would look like if it could do the following:

- Embrace a Jesus-centric mission of love, connection, and service;
- Cherish Christianity's heritage without insisting on unprovable dogma and Bronze Age legalism;
- Make a meaningful social impact;
- Have a transparent governance structure for members and leaders; and
- Have world-class operating and fundraising processes to maximize the amount of good that can be achieved for every dollar raised?

This chapter provides a few thought starters for those who believe that deconstructing and reinventing Christian churches is worth the effort. It would not be a trivial undertaking. It would require Christian leaders who are naturally loving, clear about their priorities and how they will achieve them, able to connect with different audiences, and skilled at building personal networks in their communities. It will also require people who are results-oriented, have strong communication skills, and are able to scale their churches in a Jesus-centric manner for a new age, in a new way.

CAN CHURCHES BE DECONSTRUCTED AND REINVENTED?

Christianity, Inc. is breaking down, but the old business model and the people who benefit from it are certainly not going down without a fight. Nonetheless, young people will ultimately prevail.

Transforming churches will require a new generation of theological *and* operating models. Every organizational transformation is difficult. Literalistic dogma complicates the process further because it is imbedded in membership and denominational practices, as well as in people's hearts and minds. Like every other organizational transformation, deconstructing a local church will not be able to be a "clean sheet of paper" exercise. It will be more like trying to convert an existing ranch house into a Colonial, needing to consider the already existing support structures, while also developing a new design, carefully doing the demolition work, and then rebuilding the entity in the new way.

During reinvention, a shared belief system will still be important because it will be needed to bind the congregation in a Jesus-centric way. How to measure one's Christian belief system will be covered in the section on the "Christian Snapshot" in the next chapter. On this subject, one thing to consider is the difference between "conscious Christianity" as described in this book and Christian liberalism. Liberalism uses the same theological model as Christian fundamentalism but softens many of the harsh dogmatic edges. Conscious Christianity takes this further, focusing the faith directly on love, connection, and service. Literalized dogma is seen to be an important part of the faith's formation but in many cases a barrier to its transformation.

Choosing a shared theology—while potentially difficult—will be easier than transforming the church into a well-functioning organization. There are many assets to sort through if a congregation chooses to deconstruct and reinvent itself through a conscious Christian lens. The categories set forth in Figure 8.1, "Assets for Christian Deconstruction," are intended as a starting point when considering Christian assets at the Christianity, Inc. level available across four dimensions: Individual, Social, Spiritual, and Religious.

Figure 8.1: Assets for Christian Deconstruction

Individual

Spiritual	Religious
• Embracing the Bible as the history of Christianity, through a Jesus-centric (versus Adam-based) theology based on living a Christian life with greater love, connection, and service • Prayerful meditation, Christian music, and Christian practices that give personal joy and lead to greater Christian consciousness	• Church as a place to love and connect with other Christians and help those in need in a scalable way • Emotional connection to traditions, memories, others, and what is possible in the future • The Bible as a shared devotional history of the faith for a Jesus-centric theology • Christian music and holidays as a source of inspiration during holidays throughout the year
• Shared practice with 2.3 billion Christians and the potential for spiritually activating 2,000 years of history • Established ecosystem that can support spiritual growth and community service at scale through leveraged programs and training • Spiritual path at the family, church, and community levels through the practice of meditative prayer, Jesus-centric biblical values, and shared goals	• Churches and ministers to help individuals, families, and those in need—with the scale of a small but growing fraction of 300,000 churches and $124 billion of annual revenues in the US. • Coordinated social sector programs for people during different stages of life and with specific challenges such as homelessness, addiction, abuse, hunger, and medical care • The Bible as the common denominator and source of inspiration for conscious Jesus-centric actions

Social

Within Christianity, Inc., the church is the basic operating unit, and deconstructing churches will not eliminate their need to have productive members, reliable revenue sources, good expense management, and excellent leaders and employees. Credit should be given where credit is due. Despite increasing rates of decline, the dogmatic Christian business model is very well-understood, whereas a deconstruction-friendly version of Christianity is not. To succeed, deconstructed churches will need a clear identity, effective organizational structure, solid growth strategy, good funding mechanisms, and compelling value propositions for their members and communities.

Deconstructing individual churches will require a spirit of experimentation and innovation. If churches choose to do this work, various leadership models will likely be tested, the role of the pastor as the "expert" may need to change, and hub-and-spoke logistics models may be needed to optimize the effectiveness of legacy churches that were designed as stand-alone entities.

For Christian churches to deconstruct and transform, new generations of theological and operating models will be required. Fortunately, Christianity has a lot of assets to work with. Christian traditions can still be embraced while deconstructing from the literalistic dogma that produced them. Churches can be redesigned around Jesus' priorities of love, connection, and service to others.

Regardless of how church models evolve, much can be learned from the non-profit sector more generally. Successful non-profits operate without using the threat of hell to recruit, the promise of heaven to retain, literalistic biblical dogma to control, or a repertoire of supernatural ideas to keep members united and in line. They also have objective operating success metrics. For example, Charity Navigator measures and compares 1.6 million U.S. non-profits on a variety of factors including revenue, length of operations, public support, fundraising expenses, and administrative expenses. For the benefit of non-profit donors, they measure and rank each organization's financial health, accountability, and transparency. Imagine if churches had this type of transparency, as they transformed their assets to organize social capital in a world class way.

CHURCH REINVENTION 101

What if a Christian church could be the very best in the world at efficiently and effectively using its resources to help members grow spiritually, spread love and non-judgment inside and outside their walls, and help local people who are struggling? Every congregation, like every individual, will require a different path, but here are five thought starters.

Considerations for Church Reinvention

- Embrace a Jesus-centric theology centered on love, connection, and service.
- Cherish Christianity's heritage, without literalizing its unprovable dogma.
- Focus on one or two community needs, using metrics to measure impact.
- Establish a transparent governance structure for members and leaders.
- Incorporate proven operating and fundraising routines to grow and continually improve the church's social impact per revenue dollar.

Members giving time and money still matters—perhaps more than ever. If a member has resources and the church is well managed, giving should be embraced as a human, spiritual, and moral obligation. But there is also an organizational obligation to maximize the impact of how these resources are deployed. When fundraising, deconstructed churches should be honest and not use literalistic dogma to obfuscate the giving process. Facts are friendly, and everyone should be accountable to one another based on facts.

For organizations, money is like oxygen. But giving should not be a black hole with no organizational accountability for how the money is used. Fundraising should not be about storing up "treasures in heaven" or giving to church leaders with no questions asked. Also, for at least 50% of Christians, personal giving should not be about giving money. For Christians with money, financial giving is critical. For those who cannot give money, giving time and talent is the great equalizer and essential for well-run churches to make a major difference.

Churches should be led like other successful non-profit organizations, with each church having a clearly defined purpose. When Jesus saw the crowds in Matthew 9, he had compassion on them because, as he explained, they were like sheep without a shepherd. He said to his disciples, "The harvest is plentiful, but the workers are few."

Today, people are suffering everywhere, with crime, homelessness, drug abuse, and health crises all around us. In America, when economic inequality was not as marked, tents were used for camping in the great outdoors. Today, they are used for housing people on the sidewalks of Los Angeles and other major cities across the country. Who knows, some reinvented churches may consider using their facilities to specifically help the homeless and addicted. Wouldn't this bear more fruit than some church buildings are producing today?

DECONSTRUCTING IN REAL LIFE: *"My biggest struggle is still trying to figure out what is really true. I believed something so strongly for so long that turned out to be bullshit, so how do I know I'm not fooling myself again? What if I'm wrong in a different way? All that being said, while deconstruction has been tough, it has been very rewarding being able to help others who have gone through the same thing."*

What if a church was designed around Jesus' priorities of love, connection, and service? What if churches could become the best organizers of social capital in the world? While everyone should be directly involved with helping suffering people, what if *tithing* meant money when members had financial resources and service when they had more time than money? Imagine if *everyone* in church helped those in need, with financially richer members carrying the weight financially and poorer ones helping people directly. Imagine if churches were reinvented to increase and optimize their resources in new and life-changing ways?

The traditional benchmark for Christian tithing is 10%, and this percentage is also the minimum level recommended by the secular

"Effective Altruism" movement. Today, church giving is estimated to be less than 3%. Imagine if churches were well-run and every Christian gave either 10% of their income, or 4 hours a week of their personal time, or some combination, organized through transparently governed churches that held themselves accountable for the quality and productivity of their social impact.

Serious giving is not easy, but the giver *and* the receiver both benefit from the process. Helping others leads to spiritual growth through cultivating personal generosity by systematically loosening the grip of our material attachment. Giving helps us to train our minds to resist the clinging and craving that leads to greater selfishness and suffering. Well-run Jesus-centric churches have the potential to cultivate generosity to make a more meaningful difference in the world.

Becoming a well-run church will require defining and measuring the fruit it is producing. For example, would you rather give to a church if its priority was to build sanctuaries or buy a jet, or to quantitatively transform people's lives in the local community? Is it more compelling to have more people say the sinner's prayer or to transform communities in a meaningful way? What if churches could help bring about Jesus' vision: "Thy kingdom come, thy will be done, on earth as it is in heaven."

For those interested in congregational deconstruction, it might be useful to consider various cultural shifts as shown in Table 8.1, "Deconstruction Shifts."

Table 8.1. Deconstruction Shifts

DOGMATIC CHURCH CULTURE	CONSCIOUS CHURCH CULTURE
Island-like separation	Bridge-like connection
Fear-based	Love-based
Exclusive	Inclusive
Pharisee-like	Jesus-like
Clings to dogmatic answers	Explores spiritual questions

DOGMATIC CHURCH CULTURE	CONSCIOUS CHURCH CULTURE
Judgmental of differences	Loving unconditionally
Internally focused	Externally focused
Enforces legalistic rules	Reinforces Jesus' priorities
Condemns others	Practices continuous forgiveness
Obsessive about life after death	Encourages resurrection throughout life
Dwells on the past and future	Connected to the present moment
Heaven is in the future	The kingdom within is right now
Strives to be right	Thrives through being curious

Jesus overturned tables in the temple and actively helped people in need on the streets. He did not love others dogmatically but connected with them where and when they were hurting. He showed that when people helped others, they transformed their own lives as well. All organizations have a natural tendency to focus inwardly. It's very easy for the urgent to squeeze out the important. There will always be people issues, financial challenges, work to do on programs, and day-to-day operations to manage. Despite these realities, great organizations are able to focus outwardly.

* * *

One way Jesus-centric churches could be and stay externally focused is to unite around important needs in local communities—that is, cultivated through, not done to, the communities themselves. This approach would benefit from congregational focus areas. No person or church can solve every problem, but every person and church can help at least one person in need.

There are many important local needs that churches can focus on. For thought starters, here are some identified by the Asset-Based

Community Development Institute (ABCD), an organization focused on sustainable community development.[3] Imagine if every church could make a meaningful impact with just one of these issues in their local community:

- Unemployment
- Broken families
- Gangs
- Child abuse
- Welfare
- Dropouts
- Homelessness
- Truancy
- Slum housing
- Illiteracy
- Crime
- Mental disability
- Addiction
- Sexual abuse

An important insight from community experts deserving serious reflection is that sustainable change needs to happen *through*, not *to*, people. This includes individuals, families, and communities more generally. To make a meaningful difference, time and money need to be used carefully. ABCD has shown that community strengths need to be built from the inside out to avoid many of the dysfunctions that occur from outside-in approaches. *Toxic Charity* also examined the giving process with the following conclusions.[4]

Engaging in outside-in giving without building upon strength from the inside can often cultivate feelings of superiority with givers and contempt from those in need. ABCD has found that focusing on solving problems *for* people provides immediate benefits but often leaves them

---

[3]The ABCD Institute and its available resources can be found online at https://resources.depaul.edu/abcd-institute/Pages/default.aspx.

[4]Robert D Lupton, *Toxic Charity: How Churches and Charities Hurt Those They Help (And How to Reverse It)* (New York, HarperOne, 2011).

feeling like deficient victims, outsources responsibility to outsiders, and further weakens the bonds needed for communities to function properly. Through outside-in efforts, giving can help people survive but usually does not lead to systemic change or a sustainable sense of hope.

Table 8.2. Giving and Results

OUTSIDE-IN GIVING	RESULTS
Give once	Results in appreciation
Give twice	Results in anticipation
Give three times	Results in expectation
Give four times	Results in entitlement
Give five times	Results in dependency

ABCD experts have found that building on existing assets is important to sustainably help communities from the inside out, household by household, building by building, and block by block. To make a significant Jesus-centric difference, church members should consider activating existing resources, attracting sustainable sources of funding, and personally living in the communities being served.

Neighborhood-focused lessons from effective community organizing groups, community economic development, and neighborhood planning can be used to help churches learn from others. It will also be wise to consider starting with a simpler problem area and work up to more complex problems as management and operational capabilities improve. In a one-step forward, half-step backward fashion, various people and organizations may prove to be good partners, such as the following:

Local businesses	Schools	Local mentors
Other churches	Parks	Hospitals
Community colleges	Targeted philanthropy	Libraries
Police representatives	Fire representatives	Non-profits
Government agencies	Block clubs	Cultural groups
Individual givers	Artists	Neighborhood leaders
Youth volunteers	Retirees	The unemployed

Collaboration is another important skill for people to cultivate inside and outside of the church, so that diverse groups of people and leaders can continually learn from one another, get on the same page, and productively head in clearly defined and shared directions. With needs so large, and people and organizations so varied, formal collaboration skills will be greatly needed within churches as they move from focusing inside to engaging outside their sanctuaries.

Deconstructing and reinventing a church will not be easy. It will require strong commitment and leadership. From other organizations that have been transformed, we have learned that the best leaders are open, accountable, approachable, understanding, and communicative. They have a positive ability to challenge others, give clear expectations for success, and are good at mentoring. Good leaders exude trust, respect, and honesty. They are good teachers and learners, and display empathy, and passion.

Ineffective leaders are narcissistic. They are often micromanagers, execute poorly, treat people badly, and exude negativity and reactivity. It's best to try to stay away from leaders who focus on how they look to others, take credit for successes, and shift blame away from themselves when there are issues. Consider it a red flag if a leader does not let other people make decisions and is more interested in their own reputation than in the success of their organizations.

* * *

To deconstruct and reinvent a church, members will need to step out of their comfort zones. But imagine if loving and helping people in a Jesus-centric way became an organizational core competency for 21st-century Christian churches. What if congregations were able to use the buildings that already exist to grow spiritually and lovingly rebuild local communities?

CHAPTER SUMMARY IN STORYBOOK FORM

- Once upon a time, many Christian churches lost their way, and this caused them to lose their relevance and impact.

- Every day, churches focused on defending their dogma and separated from the outside world.
- One day, Christians discovered that they could deconstruct their churches and reinvent them to help more people.
- Because of that, they began to focus on love, connection, and service.
- Because of that, churches were able to transform and make major impacts in their local communities.
- Until finally, donations and members grew again, and Christian churches became admired for the fruit they produced.
- And then they were able to live happily ever after.

9

Moving Forward

*You are the light of the world. A town built on a hill
cannot be hidden.*

Matthew 5:14, NIV

SO, WHERE CAN Christians go from here?

For me, deconstructing as a Christian was like waking up from a dream. Part of that dream was believing that literalized dogma and church business models were the foundation of the Christian faith when they were more accurately the tools of its leaders.

Christianity without dogma is not Christianity-lite: it is Christianity extra-strength. It is focused on what Jesus prioritized, irrespective of the political and cultural agendas of the day. While there is undoubtably a Christian war going on, it seems to be a political war in the hands of powerful Christian imposters in the United States and around the world. It is not a supernatural war between angels and demons.

By removing dogma, we can free the faith from its dualism, traumatic religious practices, and fear-based business models. It does not need to be used to undermine public education, democracy more generally, and the rights of non-straight white males. The man-like God in the sky that has been created by Christian leaders can be let out of its dogmatic cage. Embracing Jesus can help us show the world what happens when humanity meets divinity, when we focus on what he prioritized as most important: love, connection, and service. Conscious Christianity is as simple as it is powerful.

If Christianity, Inc. was a blue-chip stock, investment analysts would be issuing "sell" warnings. But imagine if Christianity as a loving spiritual practice could be resurrected. What if, one person and one church at a time, Christians were able to stop using dogma like weapons and secret decoder rings and focused on Jesus' priorities, all to help people live better lives. Imagine if Christianity's infrastructure could be reinvented to help more people "have life and ... have it more abundantly."[1]

The Christian torch is being passed to a new generation, and my greatest hope for people who are deconstructing is that they can help the faith forge a better path forward. It is a good time for Christians to say and do something new and stop doubling down on the faith's politicization and increasingly outdated, hurtful business models. It's good that Christians are walking away when leaders insist on hateful rhetoric and refuse to focus on what Jesus said was most important.

*   *   *

Conscious Christianity grows with more humility and uncertainty. With deconstruction, curiosity is not a sign that someone has lost their faith but an indication that their faith is important enough for them to want to question the parts that are not like Jesus' priorities. It is like what Jesus said in Matthew 7:16, "You will know them by their fruits."[2]

While this book provides a path to eliminate legalistic dogma entirely, doing this may not be practical, or even desirable, for many Christians and most churches. In retrospect, it was not my intention

---

[1] John 10:10, NKJV

[2] NASB

during my own deconstruction either. I assumed I would add dogma back in once I felt I got to the bedrock of my Christian faith. Once I removed the dogma, though, for me, it became unnecessary to add supernaturalism back in. I became comfortable with those three important words: "I don't know." As I shed literalistic dogma, I was actually able to cherish Christian traditions even more because I was no longer burdened by any unprovable theological mental gymnastics.

DECONSTRUCTING IN REAL LIFE: *"I deconstructed because of all the ways the church community was harmful to me and people I loved, and I couldn't really ignore or try to justify it anymore. However, Jesus' teachings are a core part of my life and how I try to view the world."*

Some of the biggest opponents of this book will likely be Christians who have vested personal, financial, and political interests in the Christianity, Inc. system. Christians who are most threatened by deconstruction have often lived in dogmatic Christian bubbles as far back as they can remember. They have heard church dogma preached every Sunday, seen it reinforced in every Christian book they have read, and rehearsed it in every Christian song they have sung. People employed by Christianity, Inc. have been taught what to believe, what they can preach, and have very few career options outside of their own denomination's dogmatic swim lanes. I believe that most are well-meaning people, but that their beliefs are byproducts of bad Christian business models.

Christianity without dogma is not Christianity-lite: it is Christianity extra-strength. With the unprovable dogma removed, the Christian faith can be freed from its dualism, traumatic religious practices, and outdated business models. The Christian torch is being passed to a new generation, and my greatest hope for people who are deconstructing is that they can help the faith forge a better path forward.

For people who are *not* employed by Christianity, Inc., I hope the deconstruction process can be less like a crisis of faith and more like an ongoing personal metamorphosis. One of the great things about conscious Christianity is that we can cherish many of the same things we did before, but with more honesty. As a personal example, one of my cherished possessions is a thick, well-worn, copiously underlined and notated King James Bible. My mom gave it to my dad when I was four years old, and I cannot look at that Bible without thinking about him fondly. When I read his Bible today, I interpret it very differently than he did. But reading it is meaningful, and I feel close to him as I read his many personal scribblings. It illuminates how the Bible has stood the test of time throughout my life and over the centuries. The same Bible that inspires me as someone who is not a dogmatic literalist also inspired my father, who certainly was.

DECONSTRUCTING IN REAL LIFE: *"I started deconstructing at 19. I was married to an abusive, crappy Christian at 18 but was so heavily involved in the church that it seemed normal. I was "that kid" who was on fire for Jesus. When I realized I was actually being abused, I left and started deconstructing my faith. My biggest struggle has been finding balance. I don't want Christians I used to be close with to judge me or think I have no relationship with the Lord because that isn't true!"*

Christian consciousness is a spiritual journey, not a rigid belief system. If I could go back in time and talk to the little Evangelical boy that I was in the 1960s, I would suggest that he think about Christian dogma differently. I would tell him (as I would tell many deconstructing Christians today), that Christianity without dogma can be just as Bible-based as dogmatic Christianity. Here is how I would explain it to my younger self:

1. *Bible:* The Bible is an important part of our Christian history and filled with wonderful passages, It was assembled by the early Catholic Church and painstakingly preserved by Christian organizations over the centuries.
2. *God:* God can be embraced spiritually and lovingly as the great *I AM*, love, and spirit, just as it says in the Bible.
3. *Jesus:* We can accept Jesus into our hearts as the centerpiece of our Christian practice and focus on what he said was most important in the Bible—love, connection, and service.

4. *Kingdom:* Christians can embrace the kingdom of heaven within and make earth more like heaven, which Jesus tells his followers to do in the Bible.

5. *Afterlife:* People do not know what happens after death, but we do know what is happening in the present moment. Even in the Bible there are different views. Regardless, Jesus said that God is a God of the living.

6. *Dogma:* Do not worry about or waste energy on unprovable dogma other than as a spiritual pointer. Christians who claim special knowledge are dishonest, mistaken, or both.

7. *Life:* We can love ourselves and others and live more abundantly when we live in the present moment like the lilies and wildflowers that Jesus talked about.

THE *CHRISTIAN SNAPSHOT*—A FREE TOOL TO HELP CHRISTIANS CHART THEIR COURSES

Going through the deconstruction process can be painful and confusing. Many Christians, especially women, people of color, non-heterosexuals, and non-cisgender people, have been hurt by Christian dogma and peer group gaslighting. One thing that can make it even more difficult is that there is not a common language or framework for understanding Christian belief systems. This lack of a shared framework makes it difficult for those who are deconstructing to try to explain their beliefs to others. When writing this book, I watched, read, and listened to many Christian deconstruction experiences. As I did, it seemed to me that a free, personalized, and private "consulting" tool might help people quickly look at the changes in their Christian beliefs—something like an Enneagram test, but for those who are deconstructing.

While writing this book, I created a free assessment survey called the Christian Snapshot. The purpose of this tool is to help people to quickly create a baseline for where their beliefs are at, how they have changed, and how they are different from peers. It provides a language and framework to help deconstructing Christians articulate where they are in their journey and get a snapshot of what they wish to focus on. The individual version of the survey and personalized report are available free for the foreseeable future at ChristianSnapshot.com. A sample snapshot is available in Figure 9.1.

Figure 9.1. Christian Snapshot Sample Report

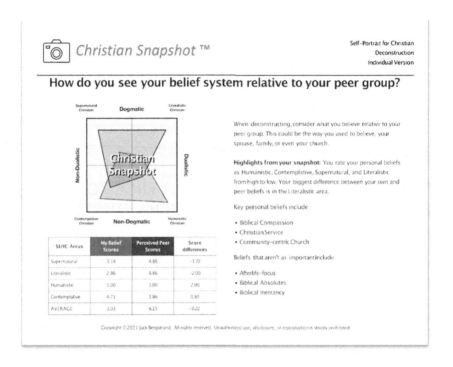

The Christian Snapshot is designed to help people create a personalized "snapshot" of their Christian belief system. The online survey can be completed in about 10 minutes, personalized results are immediately analyzed, and a report is sent to the respondent's email. The survey and report are designed to help deconstructing Christians synthesize their beliefs and compare them to their designated peer groups. These peer groups can be whomever or whatever the person taking the survey finds most useful. Examples might include their church, family, significant other, spouse, previous belief system, or any other person or group they choose to compare themselves to.

The Christian Snapshot measures and synthesizes 28 different Christian belief characteristics and provides the survey takers a picture of their personal belief system, highlights key differences with designated peers, and identifies the most important priorities they have chosen for moving forward. The snapshot maps Christian beliefs to four quadrants: Supernatural (S), Literalistic (L), Humanistic (H), and Contemplative (C) (see Figure 9.2). The SLHC snapshot can quickly help people visualize their Christian beliefs as well as their personal alignment with their designated peers around the Bible, God, Jesus, the church, spirituality, the afterlife, and Christian practice.

Figure 9.2. Christian Snapshot Belief Quadrants

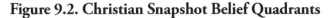

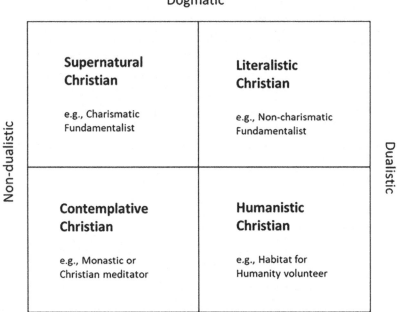

The Christian Snapshot was designed as a holon, which is something that is simultaneously a whole by itself and part of a larger whole. It therefore can accommodate that different people will have different mixtures of dogmatism and dualism at a variety of different levels. For example, someone could have general beliefs related to the supernatural, literalistic, humanistic, and contemplative quadrants, yet also have specific beliefs that differ depending on the characteristic. The Christian Snapshot model accommodates changes in beliefs over time. For example, as people deconstruct, the shifts they experience between dogmatism and dualism may change a little every time they take the survey.

In the Christian Snapshot, there are no right or wrong answers other than what the individual believes is important to them at that moment. People's beliefs, situations, and designated peers can all change over time. The four SLHC quadrants each have strengths and weaknesses, depending on the person, their goals, and their environment. The Christian Snapshot can easily be retaken whenever someone wants to reassess where they are and consider where they intend to go in the future.

The goal of the Christian Snapshot is to help people—regardless of their belief system—more quickly, painlessly, and holistically deconstruct. It does this by making it easier to visualize their beliefs, reflect on their current state, and move forward with greater confidence. Overall here are some benefits of the Christian Snapshot:

- It creates a common language and framework for assessing and deconstructing Christian beliefs;
- It improves people's ability to better understand and articulate their Christian beliefs as well as those of others and to talk about those beliefs more clearly;
- It helps people explain where they think differently from others, especially if someone's designated peer has also taken the Christian Snapshot;
- It shows people's most important priorities for moving forward.

With their Christian Snapshot report in hand, deconstructing Christians may find it beneficial to ask and reflect upon the following questions:

- How aligned is my personal belief system with that of my designated peer?

- Does my designated peer actually believe the way I had assumed?
- Given my personal results and the priorities I have chosen, what is the best way to move forward?

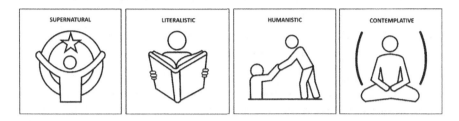

There are 15 different Christian Snapshot profiles (see Appendix), with additional variations within each of these categories. In the SLHC model, people with a Supernatural (S) orientation tend to embrace mystery, Literalists (L) embrace clarity, Humanists (H) embrace helping others, and Contemplatives (C) embrace introspection. Every Christian, regardless of their belief system, will fit somewhere in the SLHC holon. There are no right or wrong answers, profiles, or paths forward, other than what is right for the person taking the survey.

CHRISTIAN SNAPSHOT EXAMPLE: THE LITERALISTIC CHRISTIAN

One of the 15 Christian Snapshot profiles is labeled as the Literalistic Christian. This snapshot results when people have high preferences for the dogmatic and dualistic beliefs related to the Literalistic quadrant (L) of the SLHC framework.

The Literalistic Christian profile is likely to result when the person taking the survey (or designated peer) has strong beliefs in church dogma and dualistic clarity. Someone with a Literalistic Christian designation will likely have strong beliefs concerning "correct" and "incorrect" Christian behavior. Literalistic Christians tend to believe strongly in the authority of the church and supernatural dogma, including things like a physical heaven and hell, God as an objectified being, the virgin birth of Jesus, and Jesus' bodily resurrection and ascension.

This belief system is the most dualistic and dogmatic of the 15 SLHC Christian Snapshot profiles, indicating that the person values a very black-and-white Christian belief system. Literalistic Christians will tend to have strong allegiances to and trust in their church leaders and members. It can be traumatic for Literalistic Christians to deconstruct because their belief system is, or has been, very black-and-white and their peer group pressure is typically strong.

When Literalistic Christians deconstruct, they may find it helpful to embrace the deeper truths of their dogmatic beliefs. For example, they might consider reframing their supernatural dogma with a little more mystery and a little less certainty. They may also find it useful to spend more time personally helping people who are suffering and more time in silent prayer and meditation. Literalistic Christians going through deconstruction may benefit from reflecting on their Christian beliefs within and across several areas, such as the following:

- *Bible*: The Bible can be embraced as the treasured history of the Christian faith and serves as a daily source of inspiration for more than two billion Christians around the world. The religious leaders in the New Testament took scriptural literalism to an extreme, and Jesus showed that this was bad. Today, even without literalism, the Bible is a timeless and powerful resource for Christians. Jesus told the literalistic Pharisees that love fulfilled the law. Looking at the Bible through a more Jesus-centric lens may help Literalists grow spiritually as they deconstruct.

- *God*: It is possible for Christians to be in awe of a God that is beyond human comprehension or even an ability to be defined through words. Literalistic Christians can reflect on and appreciate that God is bigger than Jewish scribes were able to conceptualize, and that a more spiritual view of God is scriptural, despite the dualistic ways many religious leaders have described God over the centuries. Christians can embrace God without dogma, as the Bible itself does: as love, spirit, and as the great *I Am*.

- *Jesus*: Jesus is at the center of the Christian faith, and his message of love fulfilling the law transcended the Pharisees' emphasis on literalistic dogma. In the Bible, Jesus prioritized human love over religious law, encouraged non-judgment and human connection with others, emphasized continuously forgiving others and helping those in need. He changed the Judaic paradigm from adhering to religious legalism to loving and helping others. Jesus taught that God was here for the living and that people should live in the moment, like the lilies and wildflowers.

- *Church*: Christian churches are important to the faith and are needed to achieve many things organizationally that Christians cannot accomplish individually. The church can be used to spread Jesus Christ's love locally and around the world. Churches do a lot of good things today and can do even more by focusing on the love, connection, and service that Jesus prioritized. When in doubt, Literalists can learn from the mistakes of the Pharisees and Sadducees in the New Testament. Church dogma can point to spiritual truth without needing to be considered the literal truth.

- *Spirituality*: Like the nature of consciousness, spirituality is a mystery. There is much that Christians and non-Christians do not know with 100% certainty. What we can know through our direct experience is how to connect to the kingdom within through love, non-judgment, forgiveness, and greater service to people who are suffering. Regardless of how much literalized dogma people choose to believe, all Christians can grow spiritually by loving, connecting to, and helping others.

- *Afterlife*: The Pharisees and Sadducees in the Bible disagreed about life after death. When they asked Jesus about the afterlife, he said the kingdom of God was within and that God was a God of the living. There is plenty of work to do on earth that Christians can choose to embrace in this and every moment. We can do what Jesus told his followers to do: we can be known by our love and the type of fruit we produce.

- *Practice*: The purpose of Christianity is to help people be more like Jesus. As Christians improve their spiritual practices, they can ask: are we loving, helping others, and forgiving others enough? Are we as Christians truly engaged in life in the present moment? What can we do to model the love of Jesus more and the legalism of the Pharisees less? Like Jesus, what can we do to make the world a better and more loving place?

STATISTICS FROM CHRISTIAN SNAPSHOT SURVEYS

Deconstructionists who have taken the Christian Snapshot prior to this book's release are from the United States (76%), Europe (12%), Asia (4%), Australia (4%), and Africa (4%). Respondents were 79% female, 20% male, and 1% designated other. Reported age range was: 18–24 (25%), 25–34 (31%), 35–44 (25%), 45–54 (11%), and 55–64 (8%).

Major religious affiliations included non-charismatic Evangelical (23%), charismatic Evangelical (22%), mainline Protestant (18%), Latter-Day Saints (4%), and non-affiliated and other designations (30%). Of the respondents, 55% reported they have been deconstructing for a while, 28% are beginning to deconstruct, and 9% consider themselves fully deconstructed.

Of those who have taken the Christian Snapshot, most identified as Humanistic, followed by Contemplative, third as Supernatural, and fourth as Literalistic. The respondents' chosen peer groups were largely the opposite: first Supernatural, then Literalistic, then Humanistic and Contemplative. Respondents identified the top ten differences in their beliefs from their peer groups as (1) The importance of saving souls, (2) Biblical inerrancy, (3) Biblical absolutes, (4) Afterlife focus, (5) The church as being God-ordained, (6) A judgmental God, (7) Eternal judgment, (8) The role of the church, (9) Christian commandments, and (10) Atonement.

Compiled survey results showed that respondents' ten most important beliefs were, in order: (1) Loving kindness, (2) Jesus' compassion, (3) The Bible's compassion, (4) The church's need to help the community, (5) Service to others, (6) The church's obligation to serve, (7) God's humanity, (8) Living in the present moment, (9) Listening to an inner voice, and (10) God as spirit.

Going forward, respondents indicated they would most like to emphasize the following areas in their own lives: (1) Loving kindness, (2) Jesus' compassion, (3) Serving others, (4) Churches serving communities, and (5) Using the Bible compassionately.

SAVING THE CHRISTIAN BABY IN THE DOGMATIC BATHWATER

Is it possible for Christianity to transition from the faith of our fathers to a faith for our children? My hope is that deconstructing Christians can play an important role in helping Christianity make this shift. Deconstructing through the five Christian interdependencies and using insights from Christian Snapshot will hopefully help.

Deconstructing and improving Christianity need not be an all or nothing proposition, and one size does not fit all. I am hopeful for the next generation of the Christian faith because, regardless of how much dogma is embedded in a particular church, even the most literalistic church can choose—without changing one piece of its doctrine—to honor Jesus by loving more and judging less.

Even though this book was not written for them, someone earning their living from the Christian faith can still embrace the way Jesus fought the pious religious leaders of his day, told them to prioritize love over the law, asked them not to judge the speck in another's eye, said to give unto Caesar what was Caesar's, and showed great kindness as he helped the suffering. In this light, every church, regardless of where it is on the dogmatic spectrum, can be more like Jesus by being even 10% more loving, less judgmental, and kinder to others. It is also possible to embrace dogma a little less literally and a little more contemplatively, considering how Jesus so often described spiritual truths through his use of parables.

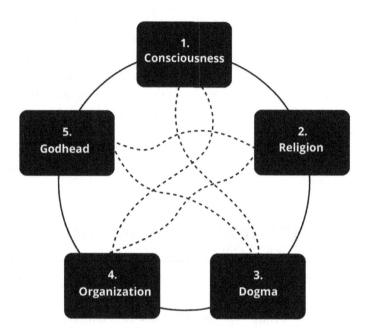

For fundamentalist atheists, like the Christians they criticize, they too can try to be 10% kinder and 10% more open to Christianity's strengths and possibilities. More than 2.3 billion people practice the Christian faith, and while not one Christian or Christian church is perfect, in most cases there is more upside in trying to make Christianity better than in trying to destroy it.

For deconstructing Christians who are actively questioning what they have been taught, I hope that some form of Christianity without dogma can help you on your spiritual journeys. Given the trends, Christian churches seem to have three strategic options. The riskiest is to try to go backwards and recapture the glory days of their "old time religion." A second path is to accept the membership declines for what they are and manage through them like every other organization does when they are in a declining industry. A third option is to build upon what is good about Christianity and transform the faith one person, church, and community at a time.

The third option does not require Christians to embrace unprovable theologies or force Bronze Age morality onto its members. Deconstructing Christians and churches can choose to reinvent

Christianity's platform, with God as love and as the great *I Am*, the Bible as the treasured history of our faith, and an organizational capability through which the world can know Christians by their love.

Based on the numbers, Christianity is on a burning platform. Unprovable dogma, traumatic practices, and political alliances are fueling the flames. For all these reasons, the deconstruction movement is an important friend of the faith, needed to help Christianity reinvent itself. Like today, various churches in the future will inevitably practice Christianity differently. If dogma remains important to a church, the choices around how the dogma is used can always be interpreted through the lens of what Jesus said was most important: love, connection, and service.

The challenge for Christianity is great, and most church leaders and apologists are not able to help because the system of Christianity, Inc. is designed to prevent them from doing so. Churches have businesses to run, leaders are paid to run them, and many leaders will use guilt, fear, and political alliances to keep people in the old system because that is all they know how to do.

But change is needed. To those who want to move the faith forward, I hope this book can help you in some small way. Wherever your spiritual path takes you and your Christian faith, I hope you will enjoy your journey, live more abundantly, and be able to become a little more like Jesus.

CHAPTER SUMMARY IN STORYBOOK FORM

- Once upon a time, Christians needed to deconstruct their core religious beliefs.
- Every day, as they deconstructed, they encountered varying degrees of confusion, emotional trauma, and ostracization.
- One day, they discovered they could grow spiritually by consciously and systematically examining their beliefs and the systems that produced those beliefs.
- Because of that, they were able to understand and deconstruct their Christian faiths better and faster.

- Because of that, they were able to shed harmful dogma and transform their lives.
- Until finally, deconstruction and transformation became as one.
- And then they were able to live happily ever after.

10

Christian Consciousness Reflections

Whatever is true, whatever is noble, whatever is right, whatever is pure, whatever is lovely, whatever is admirable—if anything is excellent or praiseworthy—think about such things.

Philippians 4:8, NIV

THIS CHAPTER INCLUDES a selection of 30 short reflections from the Christian Consciousness website.[1] Each post can be reflected upon in a few minutes, and all are organized around the five interdependencies: Consciousness, Religion, Dogma, Organization, and the Godhead.

SIX REFLECTIONS ON CONSCIOUSNESS
DAY 1 REFLECTION: Jesus taught non-duality

The mind is wired for dualism. It loves separation, categorization, and

---

[1]ChristianConsciousness.org

comparison. Examples include thinking in terms of you and me, us and them, right and wrong, past and future, and winning and losing.

Where the nature of dualism is to separate, the nature of non-dualism is to unify. Non-duality is like being able to see the forest for the trees. Jesus often spoke in non-dualistic terms. This seemed to confuse many people—even his own disciples. He used parables to bridge the gap between his non-dualistic and their dualistic thinking. There are many examples of Jesus' non-dualism in the Bible, including statements such as these: To be great, be a servant (Mark 10:43); Lose your life to save it (Luke 17:33); Rule like one who serves (Luke 22:26); Love your life and lose it (John 12:25). Jesus said, "You are in me, and I am in you" (John 14:20), "All I have is yours, and all you have is mine" (John 17:10). He asked for complete unity (John 17:23).

Jesus personified the non-dualism of being both God and man. He was in his Father and his Father was in him (John 10:38). His spiritual priorities were non-dualistic: he showed that love fulfilled the law, advocated for non-judgment of others, and encouraged serving people who were suffering. During his lifetime, the religious leaders in the New Testament were, in comparison, very dualistic. They loved their laws and the separation that gave them their status and livelihoods.

The idea of "clock time" is a dualistic concept in human life. The past and future are dualistic mental constructions, where the present moment is non-dualistic and indivisible. For example, in the Bible, "With the Lord a day is like a thousand years, and a thousand years are like a day" (2 Pet. 3:8). In Hebrews 13:1, Jesus is described as the same yesterday, today, and tomorrow.

The nature of the present moment itself is non-dualistic. Existentially, every new breath is the beginning of a new life. With greater spiritual consciousness, it can be increasingly seen that one's Christian life can only happen now. As Jesus said, "God is not the God of the dead, but of the living."[2] By transcending dualistic clock time and embracing the present moment, it is easier to understand scriptures such as those in which God tells Moses "*I AM THAT I AM*,"

---

[2]Matt. 22:32, NKJV

"Here I am! I stand at the door and knock," and "I am the Alpha and the Omega, the First and the Last, the Beginning and the End."[3]

Like the legalistic religious leaders that Jesus fought with in the Bible, our unconscious minds are also dualistic. Yet Jesus showed a new way to think and live. This was the pivot Jesus made when he set his priorities: "Love the Lord your God with all your heart and with all your soul and with all your mind," "love your neighbor as yourself," and when he explained that "all the Law and the Prophets hung on these two commandments."[4]

God is love, and love is non-dualistic. This is how Jesus taught non-duality.

DAY 2 REFLECTION: Calming the storms of the unconscious mind

The unconscious mind loves to chase conceptual storms of its own making. Rather than connect to direct experience, the untrained mind loves to engage in flurries of discursive and obsessive worries and wishes. It generates stories that keep us from living and accepting life as it is. The unconscious mind regularly and compulsively repeats the same thoughts and frets over dangers that often never materialize, replacing what is real with what is imagined.

There is an alternative to this mental conundrum. In Philippians 4:7, Paul writes about the peace of God that is beyond understanding—it comes from direct experience and living life as it truly is. In conjunction with meditation and silent prayer, conscious Christians can develop the capability to "let go and let God" and detach from the worries that the unconscious mind loves to create and cling to.

Jesus said not to worry about our lives, what we eat, or what we drink, nor for our body and what we put on. He asked his followers whether they, by being anxious, could add even one day to their lives. He asked them to be like the lilies of the field, which do not toil. Jesus said to first seek the kingdom and not be anxious about the future.[5]

---

[3]Exod. 3:14, KJV; Rev. 3:20, NIV; Rev. 22:13, NIV

[4]Matt. 22:37–40, NIV

[5]See Matt. 6

Through greater personal consciousness, Christians can relax in their uncertainties by putting their trust in the moment. Over time, as Christians we can gauge the state of our spirituality by the degree of peace we have in our minds and the love we have in our hearts.

Personal peace and happiness exist in the here and now because this is the only place where they can exist. In the Bible, Satan is portrayed as the great deceiver. This is like the role that the unconscious mind plays in our lives to keep us from embracing the abundance of the present moment. Outside of the here and now, we substitute the artificial world of discursive and compulsive thinking for true living.

Instead of chasing the storms of the mind, conscious Christians can live in peace, even when our unconscious minds are trying to tell us that we are in the eye of a hurricane. With greater consciousness, we can calm the storms of our minds and experience the peace that passes understanding.

DAY 3 REFLECTION: Contentment lives in the now

The unconscious mind loves for things to be different from what they really are. It loves to control situations, solve problems (whether they are real or perceived), live up to self-imposed ideals, and continually strive for more.

Wanting things to be different seems to make the unconscious mind feel useful. When we are sad, our minds strive to be happy. When we are happy, we think about how to keep the happiness going. When we are poor, our brains thirst for more money. When we are rich, we want to be even richer—or at least not lose what we already have.

People who think they have everything even strive to be content with their surpluses. But *striving* to be content is, in and of itself, just another act of discontentment. The unconscious mind is peculiar: it fools us into believing that happiness is always in the future. Yet, there is nothing *real* other than that which is in the present moment.

Equanimity, the Christian condition of stillness (Psalm 46:10) and the peace that passes understanding (Phil. 4:17), is the result of greater consciousness. It is what remains when we stop striving and simply belong to the moment. It is also something that happens when we let go of our unconscious mind's obsessions and calmly concentrate on our direct experience. It's like what Jesus said: "Peace I leave with you; my peace I give to you. Not as the world gives do I give to you. Let not your hearts be troubled, neither let them be afraid."[6]

By transcending the constant agitation of the unconscious mind through silent prayer and meditation, we can experience greater mental spaciousness. Once we stop pursuing the next thing, we can take ideas like success and failure less seriously. With greater equanimity, we can loosen our obsessions with *yesterday* and *tomorrow* and fully engage in the only moment we can ever have—this moment.

Expanding our consciousness through meditation, prayer, and helping others, can help us to worry less and appreciate what we have in our lives right here, right now. We can loosen the grip of our egoic minds and more fully engage in the present moment. Anchored by our breath, we can "let go and let God."

With greater consciousness, Christians can achieve without striving. When no longer striving to pursue contentment, we can know that contentment has been here all along right here, right now.

DAY 4 REFLECTION: Impermanence is our friend

Life itself is like a vapor, yet we often strive for permanence, stability, and solidity. Our minds love the notions of stability and predictability. But whether we like it or not, as the sands of time shift, and consciousness increases, we find permanence to be a human delusion. People grow old, get sick, and die. Buildings fall and societies change. Sometimes, impermanence appears slowly, and at other times, it comes quickly and without warning.

Fighting the true and transitory nature of life increases human suffering. James wrote: "Why, you do not even know what will happen tomorrow. What is your life? You are a mist that appears for a little while and then vanishes."[7] To embrace our impermanence is to embrace life itself and the preciousness of the present moment.

The idea of permanence is a mental construct. It is not the true

---

[6] John 14:27, ESV

[7] James 4:14, NIV

nature of our lives. The only permanent part of life is the present moment. With greater consciousness, we can experience the stillness of our spiritual nature and increasingly let go of the choppy nature of our egoic minds. We can experience the equanimity that Jesus spoke of: "Can any one of you by worrying add a single hour to your life? And why do you worry about clothes? See how the flowers of the field grow. They do not labor or spin. Yet I tell you that not even Solomon in all his splendor was dressed like one of these."[8]

Striving for permanence is a common egoic obsession, but spirituality can transcend it. To be a conscious Christian is to be in the state of "I am." In Exodus 3:14, God says to Moses, "I AM WHO I AM. This is what you are to say to the Israelites: 'I AM has sent me to you.'"

Impermanence is not a problem to solve. It is a friend to embrace. It is our teacher. We can live abundantly and lovingly by understanding that whatever can be lost, will be lost. Embracing impermanence can help us cultivate the wisdom of now. Of this breath. Of *I am.*

DECONSTRUCTING IN REAL LIFE: *"Even though I was practically born in the church, Hell never made sense to me, and less fundamentalistic writings I encountered always seemed truer than what I had been taught. For me, the election of Trump was the last nail-in-the-Evangelical-coffin. I have never been happier or more at peace knowing that I don't need to be certain about everything. Intellectual honesty is something that I can no longer live without, and don't need to."*

Resisting impermanence causes a perpetual state of suffering. It takes us out of life as it is and into the unconscious mind's desire to always have things be different from what they are. The practice of meditation, silent prayer, and living in the present moment can help us let go of our unconscious mind's obsession to resist life as it exists. Obsessively wanting things to be different than they are is a fool's errand. Embracing impermanence as a teacher—by letting go and letting God—can bring with it the peace that passes understanding that Paul writes about in Philippians 4:7.

---

[8]Matt. 6: 27–29, NIV

DAY 5 REFLECTION: The opposite of love is not hate

Jesus prioritized love as the greatest commandment (Matt. 22) and said, "Do not judge, and you will not be judged. Do not condemn, and you will not be condemned. Forgive, and you will be forgiven."[9]

In this sense the opposite of love is not hate. The opposite of love is judgment because judgment is the foundation of hate. To judge someone requires that we distance ourselves from them. Love comes from human connection whereas hate is fueled by separation. Judgment produces this separation, including many forms of hate-filled injustices, such as those related to religion, lifestyle, gender, sex and sexual orientation, and race. By projecting our insecurities outward, we avoid the vulnerability that comes from looking inward.

The unconscious mind is wired to separate from and judge others. It thrives on proving that we are right and someone else is wrong. Similarly, judgmental Christianity creates a culture of superiority and self-righteousness, and in the process, limits our abilities to grow spiritually and connect with others.

Unconscious Christians judge others and use Bible verses to do it. This creates spiritual blind spots. Jesus condemned this type of blindness when he said, "Do not judge. [...] Why do you look at the speck of sawdust in someone else's eye and pay no attention to the plank in your own eye?"[10]

When someone's actions bother us, rather than immediately judge them, we can also make the choice to look inward. We can ask ourselves what our righteous indignation is telling us about what we may need to work on in our own lives. Judgment often goes both ways. People who harshly judge others often judge themselves harshly as well. We can't truly love others until we can love ourselves. Similarly, we can't truly stop judging others until we stop judging ourselves. To be more loving can be challenging, but it is an important spiritual practice. As Jesus said, "By this everyone will know that you are my disciples, if you love one another."[11]

---

[9]Luke 6:37, NIV

[10]Matt. 7:1,3, NIV

[11]John 13:35, NIV

DAY 6 REFLECTION: Living in the kingdom within

Jesus challenged the dualistic nature of the religious elite and introduced the non-dualism of love fulfilling the law. He encouraged people to grow spiritually through love, non-judgment, forgiveness, and service. Jesus told the Pharisees and Sadducees that the kingdom of God was neither here nor there but within.[12]

Consistent with what Jesus said, Christians can live happier and better lives as they become more conscious and connected. By being more loving, embracing God as love and the great I AM, and integrating Christian spirituality with religious practice, the faith's impact can be greatly multiplied.

Dualistic thinking works at cross purposes with Christian love. Dualism creates religious tribes, and these tribes believe that only their church knows the one true way. Jesus said in Luke 17:21, "Neither will they say, 'Look, here!' or, 'Look, there!' for behold, the kingdom of God is within you." With every breath we experience the end times and a new beginning. In Matthew 24:34 and Mark 13:30, Jesus said that the end times would be fulfilled in the generation of that day. He said that "Some who are standing here will not taste death before they see the kingdom of God."[13] He reaffirmed, "This generation will certainly not pass away until all these things have happened."[14]

The kingdom of God exists in the present moment. It is the only place where love, connection, and religious service can replace legalism, judgment, and religious power. It was in this light that Jesus said, "A new command I give you: Love one another. As I have loved you, so you must love one another."[15]

Jesus said, "Consider how the wildflowers grow. They do not labor or spin. Yet I tell you, not even Solomon in all his splendor was dressed like one of these."[16] This is the foundation of the kingdom within: to live life right here and right now with deep appreciation. To not live

[12]Luke 17:20–21

[13]Luke 9:27, NIV

[14]Luke 21:32, NIV

[15]John 13:34, NIV

[16]Luke 12:27, NIV

in the present moment is to cling to what we have and crave for things to be different than they are. With greater consciousness, we can live abundantly in the world of direct experience, like the wildflowers.

Often credited to Solomon, the author of Ecclesiastes wrote, "There is a time for everything, and a season for every activity under the heavens: a time to be born and a time to die, a time to plant and a time to uproot,… a time to weep and a time to laugh, a time to mourn and a time to dance."[17] Paul wrote a similar sentiment in the New Testament when he wrote that he had learned how to get along happily whether he had much or little.[18]

With greater consciousness, we can live in the kingdom within. With God as the great I Am, the present moment is eternal. There is a season for everything, and that season is now.

SEVEN REFLECTIONS ON RELIGION

DAY 7 REFLECTION: Being spiritual *and* religious

Being spiritual does not require being religious, and many religious people are often not spiritually inclined. According to Pew Research findings, 27% of U.S. adults said they were spiritual but not religious, up 8 percentage points in five years.[19]

Religion and spirituality have different natures. Looked at metaphorically, religion paints the strawberry whereas spirituality tastes it. Where spirituality is like the sun (the source of light), religion is like the moon (which reflects the very same light). The natural tension is worth examining because spirituality can help keep religion from calcifying while religion can help increase spirituality's potential.

As religious organizations helped Christianity grow, they replaced the difficult-to-define nature of spirituality with the standardized routines of dogma. As a result, Christianity became less spiritual. But

---

[17]Ecc. 3:1–2,4, NIV

[18]Phil. 4:11

[19]Michael Lipka and Claire Gecewicz, "More Americans Now Say They're Spiritual but Not Religious," (Pew Research Center, May 30, 2020), https://www.pewresearch.org/fact-tank/2017/09/06/more-americans-now-say-theyre-spiritual-but-not-religious/

spirituality needs religion to be able to help large numbers of people to grow spiritually in a systematic way.

Christianity is at its best when Christians can combine the light of spirituality with the heat of religious practice. But this requires spirituality to lead the dance in the present moment from the inside out. With greater spirituality, Christians can experience the peace of God that is beyond understanding.[20]

DECONSTRUCTING IN REAL LIFE: *"Justice was the driver for beginning my deconstruction. Things like gay marriage, racial justice, how the church handled slavery, patriarchy, gaslighting, homelessness, and focusing on the afterlife instead of improving this world all led me to deconstruct my Christian faith. I ultimately decided I could love my neighbor better by being a non-Christian."*

By being spiritual *and* religious Christians can improve the quality of their lives and the lives of others. Jesus said, "You are the light of the world. A town built on a hill cannot be hidden. Neither do people light a lamp and put it under a bowl. Instead, they put it on its stand, and it gives light to everyone in the house. In the same way, let your light shine before others, that they may see your good deeds and glorify your Father in heaven."[21]

Christian spirituality is the source of the light that can help to make churches lighthouses in their communities and around the world. As we cultivate spirituality in our own lives and churches, Christians and Christianity can help a lot more people through greater love, connection, and service.

Like a dance, the point of spirituality is not to get somewhere but to become at one with the music, at one with the light. As Jesus said, "I am the light of the world. Whoever follows me will never walk in darkness but will have the light of life."[22] The healthy integration of religion and spirituality can greatly benefit Christians and Christianity.

---

[20]Phil. 4:7

[21]Matt. 5:14–16, NIV

[22]John 8:12, NIV

As Paul writes: "Do not conform to the pattern of this world but be transformed by the renewing of your mind. [...] In Christ, we, though many, form one body, and each member belongs to all the others."[23]

DAY 8 REFLECTION: Transcending greeting card love

Jesus' two greatest commandments were to love God and others. The love that Jesus showed in the Bible wasn't the feel-good type. He fed the hungry and healed the sick. Love isn't always easy; it can take us out of our comfort zones. It may be something that we need to do when it's easier to do something else.

For example, the United States has the largest economy of any country in the world. Yet, according to the U.S. Census Bureau, one in eight Americans lives in poverty. This rate increases in difficult times as the least fortunate are hit the hardest by health and economic disruptions, and as the gap between the richest and poorest Americans continues to grow.

James 2:14–17 says it well:

What good is it, my brothers and sisters, if someone claims to have faith but has no deeds? Can such faith save them? Suppose a brother or sister is without clothes and daily food. If one of you says to them, "Go in peace; keep warm and well fed," but does nothing about their physical needs, what good is it? In the same way, faith by itself, if it is not accompanied by action, is dead. (NIV)

Love can carry with it a burden, and as we become more conscious, that burden may increase. But it is a necessary burden— a loving one. It is the burden of not insulating ourselves through the we/they dualism that the unconscious mind loves to hide behind. The burden of Christian love is the obligation to be kind to and help people we know and don't know. Doing this is an on-ramp to the Christian path that leads to the kingdom within.

To truly love requires personal action. It is love that is not like mere words on a greeting card, but something more tangible. Meaningful. Useful. *Christ-like.*

---

[23]Rom. 12:2,5, NIV

We can learn from 1 John 3: "For this is the message that you heard from the beginning, that we should love one another. [...] But whoever has this world's goods, and sees his brother in need, and shuts up his heart from him, how does the love of God abide in him? My little children, let us not love in word or in tongue, but in deed and in truth."[24]

Jesus said the poor would always be among us. The need to help others is never-ending. While we will not be able to personally eliminate poverty and suffering for everyone, we can help someone, in some way, today and every day. As individuals and as a Christian community, we can act with love, the kind that might even hurt—but in a good way.

DAY 9 REFLECTION: Christian love

Jesus proclaimed, "By this everyone will know that you are my disciples, if you love one another."[25] Paul wrote that the entire law is fulfilled in keeping this one command: "Love your neighbor as yourself."[26]

How is the Christian religion doing according to this standard?

According to Barna research, there are intensifying beliefs around the world that modern religion is at the root of a vast number of societal ills. Included are concerns about those who refuse to serve people whose lifestyle conflicts with their beliefs, how religious people deal with social issues and government policies, and the use of religion to justify violence.[27]

Is this simply a public relations problem? Is there a supernatural devil at work undermining the results of public opinion polls?

For people who claim to be Jesus followers, here's what Jesus said in Matthew 23:

- You shut the door of the kingdom of heaven in people's faces;
- You travel over land and sea to win a single convert, and when you have succeeded, you make them twice as much a child of hell as you are;

---

[24]Verse 11, 17–18, NKJV

[25]John 13:35, NIV

[26]Gal. 5:14, NIV

[27]"Five Ways Christianity Is Increasingly Viewed as Extremist," Barna (Barna Group, February 23, 2016), https://www.barna.com/research/five-ways-christianity-is-increasingly-viewed-as-extremist/.

- You hypocrites! You give a tenth of your spices. But you have neglected the more important matters of the law—justice, mercy, and faithfulness;
- You blind guides! You strain out a gnat but swallow a camel;
- You clean the outside of the cup and dish, but inside are full of greed and self-indulgence;
- You are like whitewashed tombs, which look beautiful on the outside but on the inside are full of the bones of the dead and everything unclean;
- You snakes! You brood of vipers! How will you escape being condemned to hell?

There's more, but you get the point. It's clear what religion without love looks like. How can Christians consciously build the capacity to love God with all our hearts and others as ourselves?[28]

The nature of our minds influences the nature of our lives, and what happens in our lives influences what happens in the world. The quality of our behavior is a manifestation of the quality of our thoughts. When our thoughts are centered on "me and mine," we get caught in a world of selfishness, arrogance, legalistic thinking, and tribal behavior.

Peter wrote: "Make every effort to add to your faith goodness; and to goodness, knowledge; and to knowledge, self-control; and to self-control, perseverance; and to perseverance, godliness; and to godliness, mutual affection; and to mutual affection, love."[29]

Loving ourselves and others is not always easy. But Jesus showed the religious leaders in the New Testament that the source of love was not legalistic dogma. In this spirit, what if Christians more consciously practiced the 1 Corinthians 13:4–7 kind of love? The love that is patient, kind, does not envy, does not boast, is not proud, does not dishonor others, is not self-seeking, is not easily angered, keeps no record of wrongs, does not delight in evil but rejoices with the truth, always protects, always trusts, always hopes, and always perseveres kind of love. Imagine what differences we might see in our world.

---

[28]Mark 12:30–31

[29]2 Peter 1:5–7, NIV

DAY 10 REFLECTION: Mindfulness can be a Christian practice

Our minds can imprison us in worlds of thought. We can think about the regrets we have about the past, worries we have about the future, and engage in many useless mental conversations in our heads. With all these distractions, we miss the beauty of life as it truly is in the present moment.

When we are caught up in thought, we think without even knowing that we are thinking; we are consumed with clinging to what we have and crave for more. When we become at one with our thoughts, our minds can become like the storm in the Sea of Galilee in Luke 8:23–25. A spiritual promise in this story was that when the waves were choppy, Jesus slept, whereas his disciples panicked. With greater consciousness, Jesus calmed the seas. A message for each of us is that with greater consciousness, we can also calm the seas of our minds and lives.

> **DECONSTRUCTING IN REAL LIFE:** *"In my church, I experienced a manipulative, abusive, controlling environment. As part of this, I had an unhealthy, purity culture-influenced marriage that led to depression and suicidal thoughts. When I wanted a divorce, the church leaders said God would not approve. I had to go to therapy and escape the church to regain my sanity and save my life."*

Mindfulness meditation is one way to help improve the quality of our consciousness. Dedicating some time every day to get off the treadmill of compulsive and discursive thinking is a valuable spiritual practice. By watching our thoughts come and go without being caught by them, we can free ourselves by freeing our minds. This can help us experience the peace and love that Jesus Christ modeled in a personal way.

Jesus said, "Do not worry about your life, what you will eat or drink; or about your body, what you will wear. Is not life more than food, and the body more than clothes? Look at the birds of the air;

they do not sow or reap or store away in barns, and yet your heavenly Father feeds them. Are you not much more valuable than they?"[30]

With greater consciousness, we can "let go and let God," and free ourselves from the unconscious regrets and fears that distract us from the here and now. But sometimes, professional help is also required to treat unhealthy thinking. Struggling with depression is not a sign of personal, religious, or spiritual failure. According to Lifeway Research studies, 23% of pastors acknowledged personal struggles with mental illness, and 32% of churchgoers had a close acquaintance or family member who died by suicide.

When professional help is needed, it is important to get it. When we are otherwise healthy, Christian mindfulness is an excellent way to transcend our unconscious thoughts and move from a state of always wanting things to be different than they are to one of being in the present moment—from only thinking about life to truly living it.

DAY 11 REFLECTION: Bad religion produces bad morality

Religious leaders have taught that societies can't be moral without religion. While many Christians believe this, the tide is turning. Pew Research has shown that most U.S. adults no longer think it's necessary to believe in God to be moral and have good values (56%), up from less than half of respondents (49%) six years earlier. Moreover, the research shows that attitudes are also changing among religious Christians, including white mainline Protestants, black Protestants, and white Catholics.

We certainly don't need to look very hard to find moral atrocities enacted by people claiming to have strong faiths in God. The Bible is often used to justify those acts—including discrimination of nearly every kind, oppression of the weakest in society, polygamy with young girls, and religious leaders sometimes living extravagantly off the tithes and offerings of their followers, collected through hyping up fear and supernaturalism. Despite being religious, pious people can be highly immoral, demonstrating shameless degrees of religious

---

[30]Matt. 6:25–26, NIV

hypocrisy. Jesus warned about this when he addressed the religious elite: "Do not do what they do, for they do not practice what they preach. They tie up heavy, cumbersome loads and put them on other people's shoulders, but they themselves are not willing to lift a finger to move them."[31]

There is a moral code that everyone can practice with or without going to church, and Jesus explained it. He said: "So in everything, do to others what you would have them do to you, for this sums up the Law and the Prophets."[32] And if we have been wronged? Consider how Jesus responded to Peter: "'Lord, how often shall my brother sin against me and I forgive him? Up to seven times?' Jesus said to him, 'I do not say to you, up to seven times, but up to seventy times seven.'"[33]

DECONSTRUCTING IN REAL LIFE: *"Where I was raised, I was taught that colonization was a good thing. As I got older, I increasingly discovered that this was not true. Additionally, I became more and more aware of the harm being done by the church to LGBTQ persons, women, and minorities. When I could no longer ignore that the Bible was dripping with blood, I had no choice but to begin my deconstruction process. For me, leaving the church was a moral decision."*

Becoming more conscious as a Christian requires that we let go of biblically justified hate, judgment, political revenge, and selfishness. Jesus preached three main things: love (Mark 12:30–31), connection (Matt. 7:1–3), and service (Matt. 25:25–30).

Imagine if love, connection, and service formed Christianity's North Star and shared moral code.

The Bible says that grace, mercy, and peace from God the Father and from Jesus Christ will be with us in truth and love and that loving one another is not a new command but one that has existed from the beginning.[34] It also says not to imitate what is evil but what is good,

---

[31] Matt. 23:3–5, NIV

[32] Matt. 7:12, NIV

[33] Matt. 18: 21–22, NKJV

[34] 2 John 1

that anyone who does what is good is from God, and that anyone who does what is evil has not seen God.[35]

When Christians are hateful, judgmental, and selfish (the opposite of being loving, connected, and serving), they are not trying to be like Jesus. Today and throughout time, legalistic religion has not produced morality. Just the opposite. People who claim to be moral followers of Jesus need to simply start with love as Jesus' greatest commandment.

DAY 12 REFLECTION: Christianity is a spiritual practice

Some religious leaders teach that Christians are born (or reborn) through their beliefs, not through their actions "lest any man should boast." Yet, believing this way is like buying a violin and immediately declaring yourself a violinist. If you have ever listened to a beginner musician practice, you know this is not the case. Like learning to play the violin, living a conscious Christian life not only takes practice, it also is *a* practice.

The North Star of a conscious Christian practice is concentrating on what Jesus said was most important: *love* over dogmatic legalism, *connection* over judgment, and *service* for those in need over selfishness.

Here are three practices which can help Christians move toward this North Star:

1. **Being spiritual and religious.** It's not very conscious to be religious without being spiritual. It's also often not sufficient or satisfying to be a spiritual loner and not make a meaningful external impact. Both spiritual growth and religious scalability are needed to transform people's lives in a significant and sustainable way. This practice can benefit from meditation, silent prayer, and community service.

2. **Being intellectually honest.** A conscious Christian practice requires an open mind and heart, and a life grounded in direct experience. When something can't be proven, as is often the case with dogmatic legalism, we can learn from it without requiring it to be factual, and not waste time arguing about it

---

[35] 3 John 11

or trying to impose it on others. There are more than enough important things in this world that can be proven and that can benefit from our personal and congregational attention.

3. **Being socially compassionate.** Jesus led the Christian transition from law to love. He fought the legalistic religious leaders of his day and focused on helping those in need—healing the sick, feeding the hungry, and helping the mentally ill. This is a very good time for Christians to help people in need.

Christianity exists in the present moment. It is not about dwelling on the past or worrying about the future. It requires connecting to life as it exists right now. It is not about needing to be certain but about embracing life's mysteries with spiritual enthusiasm. We don't need to think we have all the right answers. We simply need to be able to ask increasingly better questions.

With practice, Christians can move the foundation of their faith from a set of unprovable beliefs (a product of the dualistic mind) and create action-oriented lives of love and service (a product of the heart). Less like the religious elite in the New Testament and more like Jesus, Christians can serve their way—not try to theologize their way—to abundant Christian living, trying to prove each day that faith without works is dead. Like a caterpillar becoming a butterfly, as conscious Christians, we can help ourselves, our churches, and our communities by practicing and doing what Jesus said was most important: loving, connecting, and serving.

DAY 13 REFLECTION: The expanding practice of prayer

As children, Christians learn to pray using words. To make it easier, some of the prayers even come in rhymes. In churches, ministers and priests also pray using words, often to direct and control the thoughts of congregations and publicly negotiate with God. These prayers can happen in free form as well as through liturgy. Spoken prayers have a place, but there is a continuum of consciousness with prayer.

Praying to God using words instead of listening for God in silence is a little like someone having the opportunity to meet the most important person in the world and then not letting her say anything. Where the religious exert dominance when they pray, spiritual people will favor contemplative prayer that is more like mindfulness meditation. They listen and watch instead of talk and direct.

Jesus called those praying publicly in the synagogues *hypocrites*. He taught that instead,

> When you pray, go into your room, close the door and pray to your Father, who is unseen. Then your Father, who sees what is done in secret, will reward you. And when you pray, do not keep on babbling like pagans, for they think they will be heard because of their many words. Do not be like them, for your Father knows what you need before you ask him.[36]

Meditation is growing rapidly among Christians. According to the 2018 Religious Landscape Study, many Christians, including 49% of Evangelical Protestants, 40% of Catholics, and 55% of members of the historically black Protestant tradition, say they meditate once a week or more. Among those who said they prayed at least weekly, 50% said they meditated regularly.

Prayerful meditation is an important part of a conscious Christian practice. Our unconscious minds are like muddy ponds that are all stirred up, and when they become still, the mud can settle, and the water can become clear. One of the joys of prayerful meditation is realizing that we are not our thoughts. We don't need to try to influence the outcome but simply be present. Rather than clinging to our thoughts, we can lovingly watch them come and go. Spiritually, through emptying the clutter in our minds, we can connect to our direct experience.

Even though Christians learn to pray by talking, it's more spiritual and wiser to transcend this. When we don't pray through words like children, we can become more conscious, and more fully engage in the present moment with greater love and gratitude.

---

[36]Matt. 6:6–8, NIV

FIVE REFLECTIONS ON DOGMA
DAY 14 REFLECTION: Dogma can be misused

Dogma, by definition, is not provable by independent parties as literal truth. But it can often point to spiritual truth. Dogma is also not the foundation of the Christian faith, even though many leaders claim that it is. It is how churches define their brands and control their congregations, much like the religious elite used "the law" to define and control Jews in the New Testament. Dogma is an unproven set of beliefs laid down by religious authorities and treated as incontrovertibly true using supernaturalism. It is used to separate inside groups from outside groups, and bind denominations, congregations, and church members. When church leaders are hateful, the way they use dogma tends to be hateful. When they are loving, the way they use dogma is loving.

With religion and politics, it is easy to see the flaws in someone else's dogma but difficult to see and admit the flaws in our own. Even within Christianity, Protestants can easily see the flaws of Catholics, Baptists of Episcopalians, Pentecostals of Methodists, etc. Sometimes the dogmatic differences are small, and in other cases, they can be significant. The use of dogma can run the gamut from providing inspiration to encouraging pathological behaviors.

A characteristic of dogma that can make it dangerous is that it does not change with new information. Since dogma is required to be accepted as incontrovertibly true by church members, often even attributed to God, church members who question dogma must either stay and believe, quit and be shunned, or join new groups with different beliefs. Adaptation has occurred in a few cases within denominations, but usually at a price. For example, there have been significant splits within the Baptist and Methodist denominations. It also occurred in a significant way through the Protestant Reformation more than 500 years ago and inspired the formation of the early Christian church more than 2,000 years ago.

Christian dogma is used in several ways. It is used to recruit and keep members, to clearly differentiate and separate themselves from competing organizations, and to generate revenue to support their causes. Leaders typically insist that only their dogma is truly biblical. However, their dogma is always the product that they are selling and the source of their livelihoods.

Christianity without dogma can be more honest, because basing the faith on unprovable dogma makes ignorance its foundation. To base our Christian beliefs on dogma is to build on a foundation of sand, not the rock of what Jesus said was most important, love, which is Christianity's greatest commandment.[37] Love needs no dogma and is, as Jesus said: "By this everyone will know that you are my disciples, if you love one another."[38]

DAY 15 REFLECTION: The Bible is like a Christian Rorschach test

Rorschach tests are psychological instruments sometimes used to assess emotional functioning. People can see very different things when interpreting similar drawings. This is true with the Bible as well. Loving people often see love where hateful people see hate. This is one reason why the same Bible can be used for good as well as evil.

Paul wrote that all scripture was given by the inspiration of God.[39] However, he was not describing the Christian Bible. After all, the Bible that we know today did not exist until more than one thousand years after Paul lived. With respect to his own writings, Paul never claimed them to be scriptural, even though they make up a significant part of today's New Testament.

The Old and New Testaments provide a well-preserved history of Judaism and the early Christian faith. Biblical writings are used in different ways by various Christian organizations, Christian leaders, and Christians more generally—for better and for worse. Even though Jesus prioritized love as the greatest commandment, the Bible has been used by Christians to judge people in hateful ways.

Jesus' message to his followers was as clear as it was simple. He prioritized love, connection, and service to others.

---

[37] Matt. 22:37–40

[38] John 13:35, NIV

[39] 2 Tim. 3:16

Love: In Matthew 22:37–40, Jesus said, "'Love the Lord your God with all your heart and with all your soul and with all your mind.' This is the first and greatest commandment. And the second is like it: 'Love your neighbor as yourself.' All the Law and the Prophets hang on these two commandments."

Connection: Where judgment requires separation Jesus taught connection through non-judgment. In Matthew 7:1–2, Jesus said, "Do not judge, or you too will be judged. For in the same way you judge others, you will be judged, and with the measure you use, it will be measured to you."

Service: In Matthew 25:40, Jesus said, "Truly I tell you, whatever you did for one of the least of these brothers and sisters of mine, you did for me.'

The Bible is the Christian faith's common denominator. How it is read, though, like the Rorschach test, often tells us more about where someone is on their spiritual journey than on what is in the book itself. When Christians use the Bible in hateful, judgmental, and selfish ways, they are not using it in a way that is consistent with Jesus' priorities.

Jesus' priorities should be the lens through which we read the Bible and practice our Christian faith. The Bible evolved centuries after Jesus lived on earth and did not exist in its current form for most of Christianity's history. The Christian faith was cultivated in people's hearts and by what they did for the least of their brothers and sisters.

Here is a final question to reflect upon. What is your biblical Rorschach test telling you about yourself and other Christians you interact with?

DAY 16 REFLECTION: How dogma can create Christian Pharisees

In a recent Gallop poll, only one in four Christians said they believed the Bible was the actual word of God and should be taken literally. About one-fourth viewed the Bible as a book of fables, legends, history, and moral precepts. The other half fell in the middle, believing that the Bible was inspired but should not be taken literally.

Is dogmatic literalism Christianity's *one true way* or an unconscious act? Dogmatists seem to take the wrong lessons away from the arguments between Jesus and the religious elite, where Jesus said that love fulfilled the law.

There are more than 200 Christian denominations in the United States alone. They all interpret the Bible a little differently—except in one respect: their church's doctrine is superior to all others. This has resulted in Christians and various Christian churches viewing the Bible in many ways. Some view the Bible as inerrant, others as inspirational, and some as religious swords.

Regardless of one's theology, the Bible is an undeniably important book. It has stood the test of time for thousands of years, serves as a common denominator for more than 2 billion people around the world, and continues to inspire millions of people every day.

DECONSTRUCTING IN REAL LIFE: *"A large part of my deconstruction was due to an abusive marriage to someone in the ministry. I didn't recognize that a large part of what I was accepting was due to being raised under a system of white, Evangelical purity culture and patriarchy. I stayed in the marriage after years of abuse because of the beliefs I was taught about divorce. Enough was enough."*

John wrote about "the Word" non-dualistically in the first verse of the first chapter of the third gospel: "In the beginning was the Word, and the Word was with God, and the Word was God." John used "the Word" as he described something that was not in a book—something that seems much closer to a state of spiritual consciousness.

Even though Christianity was created without today's Bible, the problems associated with the dogmatic battles that Jesus had in the New Testament with the Pharisees continue to this day. Pharisaic Christians have emerged in 21ˢᵗ century Christianity. They battle over Bible verses while ignoring the sick and hungry people laying outside their churches and seminaries.

Imagine if Christians were able to do a better job at reading, reflecting upon, and practicing what was in the Bible through a Jesus-centric lens. Imagine if as Christians we could use the Bible to love God with all our hearts, souls, and minds, and love others as ourselves. What if we didn't use it to disobey Jesus and focus on the specks in the eyes of others while ignoring the beams in our own?

As a point of reflection, consider how Christians have become more like the Pharisees and less like Jesus as they have become more dogmatically legalistic.

DAY 17 REFLECTION: Is sin supernatural?

Dogma about original sin has been a key part of the Christian business model from the beginning. It's based upon Adam eating fruit from the tree of the knowledge of good and evil in the Garden of Eden. As a result, everyone was born a sinner and fell short of the glory of God. Jesus was eventually crucified to bear the sin of the world because of this. Where animals were sacrificed for atonement in the Old Testament, Jesus became the ultimate sacrifice in the New Testament.

> **DECONSTRUCTING IN REAL LIFE:** *"After spending 32 years in the Evangelical church and going to seminary, I increasingly saw more cracks in the Bible. I processed this for eight years without telling others, worrying what people would think. LGBTQ discrimination and hell were key disconnects for me. Eventually, I couldn't believe any of it anymore."*

It cannot be disputed that humans are capable of evil, and that none of us live up to even our own standards. But, if we get the root cause wrong, it's hard to get the solution right. People who meditate quickly become aware of the unconscious workings of their minds and eventually recognize that they are not their thoughts. It is all very natural. We are not supernaturally cursed. We are all good people, and we are all bad people.

Sin is not the supernatural result of Adam eating a piece of fruit in the Garden of Eden 6,000 years ago. Sin is a state of unconsciousness that keeps us from being the people we wish to be. Paul wrote about this struggle: "I do not understand what I do. For what I want to do I do not do, but what I hate I do… For I have the desire to do what is good, but I cannot carry it out."[40]

There are various ways to manage what we know to be bad for us and others. Here are three ways to think about them:

1. The least conscious choice is to try to ignore our weaknesses and project them on to others instead. Jesus spoke about this type of judgmental separation when people judged others instead of addressing the beams in their own eyes.[41] Projecting our problems onto others takes the focus off us and has a way of breeding hate, contempt, and ignorance in our hearts and throughout society.

2. A slightly more conscious response is to try to forcefully push away from our sin. In these cases, we see sin as the enemy, and we try to put up a good fight against it to the degree that we are able.[42] Fighting unconsciousness in this way can help us live better lives when we are successful, but the so-called demons can often return when our defenses are relaxed. This is often the case with addictions.

3. The most conscious response (combined with getting professional help when needed) is often to lean into our unconsciousness to understand its nature more deeply through meditation and silent prayer. Not to fight, nor give in to, but to understand, learn from, and eventually make peace with our frailties. And increasingly detach from them.

Unconsciousness is nothing to be ashamed of. As John writes, "If we claim to be without sin, we deceive ourselves and the truth is not in us."[43] Since the word *sin* has largely been ruined by Christianity's

---

[40] Rom. 7:15,18 NIV

[41] Matt. 7:5

[42] Here, "evil" is anything that harms ourselves and others.

[43] 1 John 1:8, NIV

business models over the centuries, today, *unconsciousness* might be a better, less triggering term—not as a euphemism, but as a more accurate description of the problem and indicator of the resulting solution.

We have three main options. First, we can act like our own sin doesn't exist and project our guilt on to others instead. Second, we can actively fight it as if it were a supernatural enemy and risk giving it even greater authority. Third, we can learn from and make peace with it as an unconscious pattern of thought. Through meditation and silent prayer, we can increasingly reduce its grip on our lives and learn from the lessons it has taught us.

DAY 18 REFLECTION: Atheism, Christianity, dogma, and consciousness

Atheism is as complicated as theism. To be fair to atheists, it should not be the responsibility of an atheist to prove the non-existence of a God that Christians define in an unprovable way. It is the responsibility of Christians to have a provable definition of God or hold onto their definitions more lightly. At the same time, atheists have a similar problem to Christians in not being able to defend what they cannot disprove. Both paths lead into a rabbit hole of dualistic and unconscious thoughts and arguments.

Over the years, atheistic-theistic debates (catalyzed by celebrity atheists such as American author Sam Harris and English evolutionary biologist Richard Dawkins after the 9-11 attacks) have to some degree been framed up against the backdrop of two monolithic concepts. There is science, which is portrayed as being evidence-based, and religion, which is portrayed as being unprovable. The atheistic position is that people who believe in God are misguided at best and at their worst are tent-revival snake handlers, Capitol insurgents, and confession-booth pedophiles.

The ideas that science and religion are monolithic forces are both false narratives. Atheism is not monolithic, and defining it is complicated. According to 2019 Pew Research, many people who described themselves as atheists also said they believed in a higher power or spiritual force. At the same time, some of those who identified with a religion said they didn't believe in God. To put a number to atheism, 4% of American adults identified as atheists when asked about their religious identity, up from 2% in 2009. An additional 5% of Americans called themselves agnostics, up from 3% a decade ago. The demographics skew white (78%) and male (68%). Europe is more atheistic than the United States, at closer to 15%.

There are two aspects of the atheist's dilemma to consider:

Science as a shield: The very use of the word *science* has become dogmatized and politicized. The scientific method is evidence-based, and that is good. But when people cross the line and act as if theories are factual proof, they do not stay true to the scientific process that they use as an intellectual weapon. Even the most compelling scientific theories need the acknowledgment: "We don't know for sure."

Attacking as a mode of operating: Dogmatic and mean-spirited atheists cannot prove that there is no God. Since dogmatic atheists can't prove the absence of God, they can only attack the weaknesses of their opponents. This results in many witty yet hurtful talking points, at the expense of having meaningful conversations. Sam Harris, one of the most influential American atheists of the last decade, has separately advocated that groups have productive and empathetic conversations. Yet, with his atheism, he has displayed a glaring lack of empathy when attacking religion through his debates, podcasts, and social media posts.

There are two things for dogmatic Christians to consider:

Dogma as a shield: When dogma can't be proven, Christians, like atheists, need to acknowledge: "We don't know for sure." There is much that Christians can know. Holding dogma loosely doesn't mean Christians can't embrace their traditions, but it does mean that unprovable ideas should not be forced down the throats of others. After all, Jesus called the Pharisees in the New Testament blind guides and chided them for straining out gnats while swallowing camels.[44]

Separation as a mode of operating: What if Christians spent less time in their sanctuaries and more time in their communities—not to try to convert others to their dogmatic beliefs but to help feed them and improve their lives? Without the need for dogma, Christians, like

---

[44]Matt. 23:24

Jesus, can love others, connect with them, and serve people who are struggling. That is what Jesus asked of his followers.

There is a Christian advantage in the theistic/atheistic choice. It is hard for fundamentalist atheists to unite around the existence of nothing. As a result, other than hating religion, dogmatic atheists often struggle as groups to have a unifying cause, meaningful rituals, and organizational capabilities that can make a difference in the world. However, helping people in need at scale is a core competency for many Christian groups. Many faith-based organizations do great work, including longstanding and sizeable organizations like Habitat for Humanity, YMCA, Volunteers of America, and the Salvation Army.

Imagine if Christians go even further and reactivate the potential of the more than 300,000 churches in the United States to heal and feed the suffering rather than try to convert them to their church's dogmatic beliefs.

Imagine how much better things could be if atheists and Christians alike were able to acknowledge those magic words more often: "We don't know for sure."

SEVEN REFLECTIONS ON ORGANIZATIONS
DAY 19 REFLECTION: Jesus died from organized religion

Looked at objectively, Jesus did not die in service to the church. He died because of the church. This should serve as a constant reminder for religious Christians to be ever vigilant about the embedded power and potential corruption that can exist in religious organizations.

Loving churches can be wonderful places. They can help individuals and families grow spiritually, help people in times of need, and foster lifelong relationships. They can be houses of worship and places filled with love. Yet, if we aren't careful to remember some of the lessons of Jesus in the New Testament, churches can also be abusive places. While many people's lives have been helped, many others have been traumatized by Christian churches.

In the Bible, Jesus was kind to almost everyone except the religious leaders. This is striking because these were the people who, in theory, were supposed to be on the same team. Nonetheless, Jesus called them (among other things) a brood of vipers, hypocrites, children of hell, blind guides, and blind fools.[45]

Jesus said that love fulfilled the law. The Pharisees and Sadducees earned their livings from the law and were not amused. He asked the teachers of the law: "Why do you break the command of God for the sake of your tradition?"[46] Shouldn't this be an important message to every church leader today? Christians owe it to their churches to beware of the abuses of power that can come from politics, hierarchy, and pride. As was true in the days of Jesus, a red flag that the balance has tipped from spirituality to religion is when legalistic rules replace love.

In the Bible, Jesus did not join the established religious power structure as a career. Instead, he practiced his faith on the streets as he helped people who were struggling. He showed that divinity without humanity turned into piety. When the unchangeable map of dogma replaces love as a living compass, Christianity can quickly lose its Jesus-centricity. It can create churches led by leaders who value theology and power over love and service.

Even though dogma helped to build the Christian faith in ancient times, it seems to be destroying it in modern times. Using the love that Jesus modeled as a spiritual compass, shouldn't the church's role be to transform lives, not to convert people to accept unprovable dogmatic beliefs? Isn't this what a love-based Christian faith should do? Shouldn't the goal be to transform individuals, families, and communities through love, connection, and service? With a love-based faith, churches can be both spiritual *and* religious. By being both, Christians can become more human and divine.

DAY 20 REFLECTION: The business of religion

Many Christian leaders seem to tread carefully around the biblical story of Jesus and the moneychangers in John 2. In this story, as they sell cattle, sheep, and doves, and exchange money, Jesus clears

---

[45]Matt. 3:7; 23:15–17

[46]Matt. 15:3, NIV

the temple. He creates a whip and tells the sellers to stop turning his Father's temple into a market. Today, in the United States alone, the Christian industry generates $124 billion per year.[47] According to Brotherhood Mutual (2017), the largest insurer of churches in the USA, 42% of church contributions went to salaries, 18% to buildings, and 17% was lost to fraud. Only 2% went to international missions and relief programs.[48]

Every church is a business, and in the case of Christianity, churches are often poorly run businesses. But there are no inherent reasons that churches and the broader Christian ecosystem couldn't be more effective and efficient as organizations. Imagine if churches were consciously structured to operate in world class ways to help people inside and outside their sanctuaries.

Christian organizations, like every other business, need to pay employees, run programs, build facilities, and buy lightbulbs. To do this, churches need revenue, which mostly comes from tithes and offerings. Like any other business, churches need leaders, staff, infrastructure, and marketing to operate.

Many faith-based organizations do great work and have strong organizational capabilities. But there are reasons to be concerned beyond the Brotherhood Mutual statistics. Supernaturally supercharged and prosperity gospel factions can be particularly problematic. In business, if an organization takes money from someone after promising goods or services that they then do not provide, this is a criminal act. But this kind of accountability doesn't exist within religious organizations. If people are told they can be healed through a faith offering, and then they don't get healed, leaders keep the money anyway. Oh well, God must have had other plans. If they are told that their church gifts will be multiplied and they are not, well, God will probably make it up to them later.

---

[47] Anna Miller, "Religious Organizations in the US—From the pulpit: Renewed incomes are expected to boost donations, but attendance will likely continue declining," US Industry (NAICS) Report 81311, August 2020. IBISWorld. https://www.ibisworld.com/united-states/market-research-reports/religious-organizations-industry/

[48] Brotherhood Mutual provides a number of financial resources to Christian Ministries. Although the 2017 report mentioned is not currently online, current reports can be found at https://www.brotherhoodmutual.com.

Christian charlatans commit terrible organizational abuses, and their abuses reflect poorly on Christianity overall. Using their corrupt business models, high-profile Christian leaders live lavish personal lives funded by their flocks. As the sick continue to suffer and the poor continue to struggle, charlatans buy jets and mansions and never stop asking for more. As Jesus said, "By their fruit you will recognize them."[49]

Imagine if Christian churches chose to become operationally excellent and reactivate their infrastructures in the spirit of faith without actions being dead. Imagine if Christian churches reinvented themselves around Jesus' love, connection, and service to the sick and hungry. What if every church could become a world class organizer of social capital to help people spiritually and physically and be known within every community by these fruits?

DAY 21 REFLECTION: Can Christian churches cultivate equanimity?

Christian churches rarely focus on equanimity. It is often considered a Buddhist thing, but it is very Christian, like the peace that Paul wrote about: "And the peace of God, which surpasses all understanding, will guard your hearts and your minds in Christ Jesus."[50]

We become more equanimous when we can let go of our unconscious mind's compulsions to cling to what we have and crave for more. Said another way, equanimity is the ability to let go and let God. It is a condition of perfect balance, something like a car that is in neutral gear. When things are going well, we can watch and appreciate what's happening without letting it go to our heads. When things are going poorly, we don't have to pile grief on top of it, knowing it will pass.

Without equanimity we cannot fully appreciate the present moment. We become imprisoned by our unconscious minds, want what we don't have, and constantly compare ourselves to others and to

---

[49]Matt. 7:20, NIV

[50]Phil. 4:7, NRSV

self-imposed and externally imposed standards. Making the transition to equanimity requires practice through meditation and silent prayer.

Without training and practice, the unconscious mind will always want to be in charge. The mind is a problem-solving machine, and if there's not an immediate problem to solve, it will have no trouble manufacturing a new one. When this happens, we cannot fully experience the peaceful abundance of our direct experience in the present moment.

Conscious Christian churches can help their members free themselves from their mind's obsessions and compulsions—even if only for short periods—by teaching and encouraging meditation and silent prayer. The result? Greater calmness, more personal composure, and less anxiety in Christian lives, especially during difficult times.

Equanimity increases when we can detach from the unconscious mind's seeming addiction to obsessive thinking. By loosening the grip of the egoic mind, we can directly experience the magnificence of life. Paul pointed to this in the following way: "May the God of hope fill you with all joy and peace as you trust in him, so that you may overflow with hope by the power of the Holy Spirit […] so that I may come to you with joy, by God's will, and in your company be refreshed. The God of peace be with you all."[51]

If churches can embrace and teach the path to equanimity, they will help Christians experience continuous spiritual rebirth. As it says in Second Corinthians, "If anyone is in Christ, the new creation has come: The old has gone, the new is here!"[52]

DAY 22 REFLECTION: Sin as unconsciousness

The idea of original sin has been an important part of the Christian business model from the beginning, and it continues to fuel judgmental fervor with many fundamentalists today. It is based on the story of Adam eating a piece of fruit in the Garden of Eden, God cursing humanity because of it, and Jesus ultimately dying on the cross to settle the score.

---

[51] Rom. 15:13,32–33, NIV

[52] 2 Cor. 5:17, NIV

Imagine if churches could separate the idea of sin from the story of Adam eating a piece of forbidden fruit. Does sin need to be something that controls us supernaturally, or is it a human condition that can be treated naturally?

How should churches address right from wrong? On these questions, 50% of Evangelical protestants said they believed that what was right and wrong was absolute. Mainline protestants believed it was more situational (with absolutists at only 32%). Mormons and Jehovah's Witnesses were more absolute with respect to sin, at 57%, and Catholics less absolute, at 30%.[53]

Paul wrote that "the wages of sin is death, but the gift of God is eternal life in Christ Jesus our Lord."[54] But what is the true nature of what people have called sin through the ages? What is the nature of death? Does sin affect life as we live it, or is it only cosmically important after people take their last breaths?

The concept of original sin is a dogmatic belief that is unprovable, has been misused by churches to control others and make money, and does a bad job at explaining why evil exists and how to treat it. Given these factors, the idea of original sin, other than metaphorically, is often unneeded and unhelpful in Christian organizations. Evil can just as easily be explained through examining the unconscious mind. With greater consciousness comes less sin. With less consciousness, we experience greater challenges.

One way to conceptualize sin as unconsciousness through a Christian lens is by examining the ego, dishonesty, and speck-finding.

First, there is the ego: When we are unconscious, sins of the ego are likely to occur, including the mind's compulsion to think first and foremost about *me, my,* and *mine.* The unconsciousness of greed is connected to the ego: the egoic mind always wants more. This selfishness leads to separation, as Paul wrote: "Do nothing out of selfish

[53]"Religion in America: U.S. Religious Data, Demographics and Statistics," Pew Research Center's Religion & Public Life Project, September 9, 2020, https://www.pewforum.org/religious-landscape-study/belief-in-absolute-standards-for-right-and-wrong/

[54]Rom. 6:23, NIV

ambition or vain conceit. Rather, in humility value others above your-selves."[55] With greater consciousness comes less egotism.

Second, there is dishonesty: Lying is another sign of uncon-sciousness. Not only do we lie to others, but we also lie to our-selves. Paul wrote, "Do not lie to each other."[56] Jesus said, "You will know the truth, and the truth will set you free,"[57] Unfortunately, the unconscious mind loves to generate self-serving stories that often encourage people to prefer believing in lies rather than wanting to admit being wrong. With greater consciousness there is less dishonesty.

Third, there is speck-finding: Judging others is another product of the unconscious mind. When we judge others, we take the focus off our own issues and project our judgments onto others. As Jesus said, "Why do you look at the speck of sawdust in your brother's eye and pay no attention to the plank in your own eye?"[58] Through greater consciousness, we can see more clearly how the unconscious mind generates toxic judgments quickly and often. With more conscious-ness comes more introspection and curiosity.

Thousands of years ago, the unprovable doctrine of original sin may have been a good hypothesis for its time. But today, we can stop seeing human failings as something supernatural and start seeing them as something very natural. Sin is not something to be supernaturally settled for after death but is important to address in life as part of our meditative practices in the present moment. As Jesus said, "Behold, the kingdom of God is within you."[59]

DAY 23 REFLECTION: Can Christian churches grow again?

A 2019 Gallop study found church membership had declined sharply from 70% in 1999 to only 50% twenty years later, and these

---

[55]Phil. 2:3, NIV

[56]Col. 3:9, NIV

[57]John 8:32, NIV

[58]Matt. 7:3, NIV

[59]Luke 17:21, KJV

headwinds are expected to get worse because each generation has found Christianity to be less relevant than each preceding generation. These declines span across Protestants and Catholics, genders, age groups, races, geographies, education levels, political parties, ideologies, and marital status.

Church membership is declining because every organization declines when what they used to do no longer matches what they need to do. So, what would have to be true for Christian churches to grow again?

One possible solution is for churches to become more relevant by being more Jesus-centric. Imagine if *your* church could use its organizational capabilities to focus on what Jesus said was most important: love, connection, and service. Imagine if it could transcend what the religious elite in the New Testament thought was most important: dogma, religious hierarchy, and inward-looking rituals.

Is it possible for churches to successfully shift from doctrinal conformance to personal, community, and societal transformation? What if the church's focus, like Jesus, was on feeding the hungry, healing the sick, and loving the unloved? What if members became more spiritual through silent prayer, meditation, and by helping others?

Churches can help their members achieve together what they can't achieve as individuals. When the apostle Paul helped to create the Christian church, he saw it as a spiritual body with Jesus as the head. He wrote that from Jesus, the whole body, joined and held together by every supporting ligament, grows and builds itself up in love as each part does its work. If Jesus is the head, and Jesus said love was most important, doesn't it follow that love would be the most important purpose of the church?

What would need to happen for Christian churches to be more conscious, loving, connected, and less judgmental, political, and separated? Consider a framework of four biblically supported qualities.

First, a shared vision through a lens of Christ: We can do all things through Christ who strengthens us (Phil. 4:13).

Second, clear priorities through a lens of love: We can love God with all our hearts, souls, strength, and minds; and our neighbors as ourselves (Luke 10:27).

Third, a spiritual practice of meditation and silent prayer: We can meditate upon God's unfailing love (Psalm 48:9) and his precepts and ways (Psalm 119:15). By *being* instead of *becoming* in the world, we will not be imprisoned by it (John 17:16).

Fourth, collective service for those in need: In the Bible, Jesus said,

> For I was hungry, and you gave me something to eat, I was thirsty, and you gave me something to drink, I was a stranger and you invited me in, I needed clothes and you clothed me, I was sick and you looked after me, I was in prison and you came to visit me. Truly I tell you, whatever you did for one of the least of these brothers and sisters of mine, you did for me. (Matt. 25:35–40, NIV)

Many churches serve their communities with outreach programs. Imagine if these efforts went from being a wing on the Christian house and became the foundation of the Christian house.

The trends for Christian churches are not good. But are these trends unavoidable? Imagine if Christian churches could reinvent themselves and be the very best at helping their members and communities achieve what Jesus prayed in the Lord's prayer (Matt. 6:10) and help to make Earth a little more like heaven.

DAY 24 REFLECTION: We serve; therefore, we are.

To be more conscious is to be more connected to our direct experience by living life as it is, instead of as a cacophony of thoughts. Behaviors such as looking past the homeless, justifying systemic racism, and using prisons as social holding tanks are all signs of unconsciousness.

In the same ways that Jesus focused on helping the poor and least powerful and commanded his followers to love others, wouldn't it naturally follow for Christian churches to be leading voices for helping the disadvantaged? Unfortunately, results from Pew Research on attitudes about aid for the poor have shown that as people become more religious, they are more likely to believe that aid to the poor does more harm than good. The difference is remarkable. Of those who strongly believe in God (with Evangelical Protestants and Mormons among the top), 69% think aid does more harm than good versus 6% of atheists who feel that way.

To some degree, this belief can be explained by the strong alliance between right-wing Evangelicals and right-wing Republicans in the United States. Still, it remains odd for leaders who claim to be Jesus followers to be so different from Jesus (and to instead be much more like the Pharisees were portrayed in the New Testament). Through a spiritual lens, wasn't the biblical miracle of the five loaves and two fish in the New Testament not that Jesus turned a small amount of food into a surplus, but rather that 5,000 people were no longer hungry? The contemplative yet action-oriented life of Jesus was strongly defined by his personal service to the poor, sick, and least powerful, and his simultaneous opposition to the selfishness of the rich and powerful.

Jesus said that the two greatest commandments were to love God and to love one another. Jesus' love produced actions that helped suffering people where they lived. In the second chapter of the Book of James, there are important verses for Christians and Christian churches to ponder:

> What does it profit, my brethren, if someone says he has faith but does not have works? Can faith save him? If a brother or sister is naked and destitute of daily food, and one of you says to them, "Go in peace; keep warm and well fed," but does nothing about their physical needs, what good is it? In the same way, faith by itself is dead if it is not accompanied by action. [...] As the body without the spirit is dead, so faith without deeds is dead. [60]

For Christian churches to become more conscious, what if the focus shifted toward what Jesus prioritized as most important: love, connection, and service? No one can solve every problem and help every person, but everyone can do something to help someone, and everyone can live with a greater spirit of compassion and kindness. With greater compassion and kindness, and greater relevance, perhaps Christian churches can become more conscious and begin to grow again.

---

[60]James 2:14–17,26, NKJV

DAY 25 REFLECTION: Today is the day...

Today is the day. Now is the time.

As Christian churches become more conscious and move from their conceptual dogmatic beliefs toward systematically helping people live better lives, their frames of reference will increasingly be able to move into the present moment. As David wrote, "This is the day the Lord has made; we will rejoice and be glad in it."[61]

Christianity that is unconscious, like the unconscious mind itself, is preoccupied with its dogmatic thinking. With greater consciousness, we can learn that we are not our thoughts and that thoughts are often not our friends. Developing a more Jesus-centric Christian practice through meditation and silent prayer in church can help to cultivate the ability to live with equanimity in the present moment and to experience the "peace that passes understanding" that Paul wrote about in Philippians.[62]

To experience more abundant Christian lives through greater Christian consciousness, churches may find it useful to reflect upon the following questions:

- To what degree is the Christian life a dogmatic versus a spiritual experience?
- How much of Christian practice should happen inside versus outside the church?
- To what degree should the Christian community focus on denominational dogma compared to Jesus' priorities of love, connection, and service?
- How well-connected are Christians to their direct experience and that of their communities?

Increasing Christian consciousness isn't hard, but it does take practice. Different people will take different paths, but dedicating time to personal meditation and silent prayer, engaging in a community of other like-minded and loving people, and deliberately serving (financially and physically) those who are suffering, are all good places start.

---

[61] Psalm 118:24, NKJV

[62] Phil. 4:7

What if Christians considered asking different and better questions which focused on the three things that Jesus said were most important (love, connection, and service)? Perhaps this might help Christians and the Christian church move from focusing on what dogma they believe to the best ways to love others. As Jesus said, they will know us by our fruits.[63]

Today is the day. Now is the time.

FIVE REFLECTIONS ON GOD

DAY 26 REFLECTION: But there for the grace of God...

The English reformer, John Bradford, was credited for saying, "But there for the grace of God go I" in the middle 1500s. Centuries later, Christians still say similar things. Most are expressions inserted into conversations when well-meaning people don't know what else to say, such as phrases like "God works in mysterious ways" when visiting hospitals and attending funerals. Statements like these are often attempts to harmonize a world filled with pain and uncertainty and a belief in a sovereign God who controls everything.

Conceptualizing God as a micromanaging being in the sky can cause several problems. In ancient times, it was no doubt easy to describe God in these terms, just as it was easy to believe that the earth was flat, heaven was above, hell was below, and that the sun moved around the Earth as the center of the universe.

We can biblically think about the nature of God in many ways. In John 4:24, Jesus said that God was spirit and that we are to worship in the Spirit and in truth. In 1 John 1:5, God is conceptualized as light, and it is further explained that in him is no darkness. In 1 John 4:15, the Bible says we have come to know and to believe the love that God has for us. Here, God is conceptualized as love, and whoever abides in love abides in God, and God abides in them.

Even though it's common for religious leaders to act like they have the definition of God all figured out, it is probably wiser for

---

[63]Matt. 7:20

deconstructing Christians to stop trying to describe the nature of God in words or to think about God physically as a European male, like Michelangelo did. We should also see a big red flag waving when a religious person claims to speak for God and asks people to do something for them in God's name.

Conventional Christian dogma seems to get God backwards. Genesis 1:27 says, "God created man in his own image; in the image of God, he created him; male and female he created them."[64] This infers that humanity is spiritual, not that God is physical.

While several authors of Biblical passages certainly describe God in physical forms, the Bible also says that God is spirit, God is light, and God is love. When tragedies and blessings happen in our lives, conceptualizing God as spirit makes more sense than physical depictions. Life's circumstances in this sense are not "God things." God as *I AM* and spirit, light, and love are not descriptions of a God that is micromanaging our daily lives or picking winners and losers.

In early biblical times, God was considered too vast to be described in words. If Christians today need to use a word to describe an undefinable God, then, given Jesus' greatest commandment, why not try "love?"

DAY 27 REFLECTION: Embracing God beyond words

It's curious that so many Christians seem so sure about a God that they are so unsure about. Good definitions have explanatory power, yet many definitions for God are unable to explain anything. For example, he is sovereign except when he chooses not to be. He is loving except when he's not. He is forgiving except when he isn't and is simultaneously portrayed in the Bible in a variety of contradictory ways.

Biblical descriptions of God are reflected in the times and cultures of when the passages were written. In churches, God is described in ways that are consistent with their organizational business models. A question for Christians to therefore reflect on is: if God is infinite (e.g., omniscient, omnipotent, and omnipresent), how can human

---

[64]NKJV

words, pictures, and concepts possibly be used to describe this universal lifeforce?

In art, God is often depicted as a powerful European-looking manlike being. This is not surprising since the Catholic church was based in Europe. The Sistine Chapel's *The Creation of Adam* was created not because Michelangelo had an inside track on what God looked like, but because he had to paint something, and this was what he decided on.

In the Old Testament, in Genesis 1:27, the Bible says that God created man in his own image. With the Bible as our guide, there seems to be a pretty big difference between being created in God's image as spiritual beings and what people have done over the centuries to recast God into a human image that is often used by religious leaders to manipulate their flocks and judge people.

In the New Testament, God is described as love (1 John 4:16). Still another way the Bible portrays God—in the same sense as God being love—is through David's love story to God in Psalm 23. Here, the qualities of God are those of abundance, stillness, restoration, comfort, goodness, and mercy.

Even when we choose to quote the Bible to describe God, the words themselves will inevitably fail us. They clarify and at the same time obscure. This problem illuminates why Christians should be skeptical of those who claim they can describe or speak for God with self-proclaimed authority. When religious leaders try to do this, they mislead people, and sometimes deliberately try to manipulate them.

The Bible says that God is spirit and is to be worshiped in spirit and truth.[65] Jesus spoke of this spiritual interconnection when he said that the Father was in him and he was in the Father.[66] Paul also described this human–spiritual interconnection when he wrote that there is neither Jew nor Gentile, slave nor free, male nor female; that we are all one in Christ Jesus.[67]

With greater consciousness, Christians can more directly experience

---

[65]John 4:24

[66]John 10:38

[67]Gal. 3:28

these interconnections. As Christians we can love the spirit of God with all our hearts, at a level beyond the limitations of words.

DAY 28 REFLECTION: GOD IS THE GOD OF THE LIVING

Christian business models have capitalized on the fear of God and the dread of dying over the centuries. Dogma that cultivates the fear of God, hell, and eternal judgment has been effectively used to motivate children and adults alike to adhere to church teachings.

As Christians become more conscious, these fear-based business models can be deconstructed using the Bible itself. In Matthew, Mark, and Luke, Jesus said that God was not the God of the dead but of the living.[68] Looked at through a spiritual lens, the nature of God is not "out there" but "in here." Not for another time, but for this moment. God does not need to be feared like an all-powerful tyrant but can be loved as the ultimate Alpha and Omega of spiritual continuity.

The idea of an omniscient, omnipotent, and omnipresent God is beyond human conceptualization. Indeed, the writers in the Bible described God in a variety of ways themselves, from many different perspectives. For example, John the Apostle recorded that Jesus said, "God is spirit, and his worshipers must worship in the Spirit and in truth."[69] John the Evangelist goes on to say that "whoever does not love does not know God, for God is love."[70] So, embracing God as love and spirit instead of as the man in the sky on a throne can be a good way to embrace God's nature, especially since Jesus prioritized love as the greatest commandment.

While the nature of God can't be described in words, how Christians conceptualize God can still be an important part of a conscious Christian practice. We can act as Christians, guided by God as love and spirit right here, right now. Wouldn't this be a more conscious and Jesus-centric way than fearfully conceptualizing God as a man-like object in space? To embrace God as an objectified Old Testament

---

[68] Matt. 22:32, Mark 12:27, Luke 20:38

[69] John 4:24, NIV

[70] 1 John 4:8, GNT

being encourages people to take Bronze Age morality seriously. For example, consider passages that portray God as thinking slavery and selling daughters are okay (Exod. 21), and as approving the death penalty for torn clothes (Lev. 10).

The Bible can easily be used to embrace God as the God of this moment, of spirit, and of love. God does not have to be conceptualized as an all-powerful and unpredictable creature helping those he likes and hurting those he doesn't. In spirit, God is not an objectified being. In this sense, God is closer to the idea of pure presence and pure love. With greater consciousness, we can see and celebrate that we are made in God's image as spiritual creatures.[71]

In John 4:24, Jesus said we must worship God in the Spirit and in truth. In Spirit and truth, we can be present for life as it is right here right now. We don't need to cling to the past or live in the future. *Now* is in this sense eternal. With greater consciousness, rather than being victimized, we can live lives of love and joy inspired by God as love and truth.

DAY 29 REFLECTION: Let go and let God

The past and future, as real as they may seem to us, are mental constructions. The present moment is all that there truly is and can ever be. God, like life itself, can only exist in the present moment. The unconscious mind loves to obsess about the past and future, but our breath is our anchor to this moment and to God. Therefore, *letting go and letting God* is a conscious Christian practice, which can be strengthened through meditation and silent prayer.

Barna research found that prayer was the most common spiritual practice among Americans, irrespective of their religious affiliation or non-affiliation. The most common motivation for prayer was "gratitude and thanksgiving" (62%). Other popular motivations were the "needs of their family and community" (61%), followed by "personal guidance in crisis" (49%).[72]

But what if prayer transcended negotiation? What if it was less about our hopes and fears? Less about the past and future, and more

---

[71]Gen. 1:27

[72]"Silent and Solo: How Americans Pray," Barna (Barna Group, August 15, 2017), https://www.barna.com/research/silent-solo-americans-pray/.

connected to God in this moment? What if prayer was more about spiritual stillness than hearing ourselves talk and fulfilling our personal desires? What if it was less in our heads and more in our hearts?

When Jesus retreated to pray, it's hard to imagine him talking aloud for 40 days straight. Similarly, today, silent prayer and meditation can be anchored in our breath and connected to our direct experience. In Genesis, the Lord breathed into Adam's nostrils the breath of life.[73] Through this act, Adam became a living being. Connecting to our breath can similarly help us connect to life in the present moment. The body is said to be the temple of the Holy Spirit (1 Cor. 6:19), and in this temple, our breath is its sanctuary. As in Job 32:8, it is the spirit in a person, the breath of the Almighty, that gives understanding.

DECONSTRUCTING IN REAL LIFE: *"I began to deconstruct because the theological gymnastics I had to go through became very tiring. I needed to untangle my faith from harmful beliefs like racism, homophobia, destroying the land, denying science, and being silenced and shamed as a female. I have discovered that it's okay to be okay with questions and a sense of mystery. Safe spaces are great places. While deconstruction can be hard, I'm very grateful for it."*

Letting go and letting God through meditative prayer can bring with it the peace that passes understanding. In our day-to-day lives, much of the turmoil we experience happens in our minds, which are naturally wired to obsess about the past and future. By freeing ourselves from the compulsions of our minds, we can experience more peace, generosity, patience, wisdom, truth, and love.

Paul wrote that we should not be conformed to the world but that we should be transformed by the renewing of our minds.[74] Meditation and silent prayer are ways for us to renew in each moment. When transcending thought, we can let go and let God and discover where divinity and humanity meet in our own lives right here, right now.

We simply need to breathe and engage.

---

[73]Gen. 2:7

[74]Rom. 12:2

DAY 30 REFLECTION: Is Jesus in heaven out there or in spirit right here?

The Lord's prayer is and has been often prayed in sanctuaries and homes throughout Christendom. There are many translations, but here's one:

Our Father in heaven, hallowed be your name,
Your Kingdom come, your will be done on earth as it is in heaven.
Give us today our daily bread.
Forgive us our debts, as we also have forgiven our debtors.
And lead us not into temptation but deliver us from the evil one.
For thine is the Kingdom, and the power and the glory forever, amen.

The Lord's prayer can be interpreted dualistically or non-dualistically, and the difference between the interpretations can be spiritually significant. Dogmatic Christians are raised dualistically in the Christian faith. With the Lord's prayer, the kingdom of God is "up there" in heaven, and we are "down here" on earth, and we need to make sure we go "up there" when we die and not end up in hell with the evil one.

Looked at non-dualistically, the Lord's prayer can be embraced very differently. It does not need to be about separation and can beautifully connect our mind, heart, spirituality, religion, and the world itself.

What the Lord's prayer means non-dualistically is consistent with Jesus' priorities of love, connection, and service:

1. We have an obligation to help our communities: *On earth as it is in heaven*
2. We need to focus on the present moment: *Our daily bread*
3. Forgiveness is essential to our spiritual growth: *For others and ourselves*
4. We need to train our unconscious minds: *Delivering us from temptations*

The Lord's prayer encourages us first and foremost to *serve* (do on earth as it is in heaven). We can achieve this through *being present* (focusing on today), *forgiving* (an essential ingredient for love as the greatest commandment), and being more *conscious* (letting go of the mind's egoic dysfunctions).

To put it on a T-shirt, the Lord's prayer is to bring heaven to earth, for others and ourselves. We can do this by serving, being present, forgiving, and being more conscious. These are all important ways for Christians to create a better world and live more abundant lives, consistent with cultivating the love that Jesus said fulfilled the law.

Appendix

Christian Snapshot
Profile Descriptions

THE CHRISTIAN SNAPSHOT PROVIDES DECON-STRUCTING CHRISTIANS WITH THE FOLLOWING:

- a shared framework, language, and process for individuals and small groups to use to think about and discuss their Christian journey;
- a means to more productive and meaningful conversations with Christian peers;
- a holistic way to create an integrated approach for the future;
- a structure to help make the Christian deconstruction process clearer, less anxiety-inducing, and more personally and spiritually fulfilling.

THE FIFTEEN CHRISTIAN SNAPSHOT PROFILES:

SINGLE-THREADED CHRISTIAN SNAPSHOTS	
Supernatural Christian (S)	Strong personal beliefs in the dogmatic and non-dualistic orientations of the SLHC framework.
Literalistic Christian (L)	Strong personal beliefs in the dogmatic and dualistic orientations of the SLHC framework.
Humanistic Christian (H)	Strong personal beliefs in the dualistic and non-dogmatic orientations of the SLHC framework.
Contemplative Christian (C)	Strong personal beliefs in the non-dualistic and non-dogmatic orientations of the SLHC framework.

DOUBLE-THREADED CHRISTIAN SNAPSHOTS	
Fundamental Christian (SL)	Strong personal beliefs in the Supernatural and Literalistic orientations (dogmatic) of the SLHC framework.
Structured Christian (LH)	Strong personal beliefs in the Literalistic and Humanistic orientations (dualistic) of the SLHC framework.
Pragmatic Christian (HC)	Strong personal beliefs in the Humanistic and Contemplative orientations (non-dogmatic) of the SLHC framework.
Christian Mystic (SC)	Strong personal beliefs in the Supernatural and Contemplative (non-dualistic) orientations of the SLHC framework.
Supernatural Humanist (SH)	Strong personal beliefs in the Supernatural and Humanistic orientations of the SLHC framework.
Theological Contemplative (LC)	Strong personal beliefs in the Literalistic and Contemplative orientations of the SLHC framework.

TRIPLE-THREADED CHRISTIAN SNAPSHOTS	
Doctrinal Samaritan (SLH)	Strong personal beliefs in the Supernatural, Literalistic, and Humanistic orientations of the SLHC framework.
Structured Contemplative (LHC)	Strong personal beliefs in the Literalistic, Humanistic, and Contemplative orientations of the SLHC framework.
Spontaneous Contemplative (SHC)	Strong personal beliefs in the Supernatural, Humanistic, and Contemplative orientations of the SLHC framework.
Religious Mystic (SLC)	Strong personal beliefs in the Supernatural, Literalistic, and Contemplative orientations of the SLHC framework.

QUADRUPLE-THREADED CHRISTIAN SNAPSHOT	
Christian Seeker (SLHC)	Strong personal beliefs in the Supernatural, Literalistic, Humanistic, and Contemplative orientations of the SLHC framework.

Glossary

ABCD: Asset-Based Community Development Institute, partnered with and housed at DePaul University in Chicago, Illinois.

Academic: A person who is the expert in a subject at the level of ideas, such as a professor in a college or a theologian in a seminary.

Adam-based theology: A theological model for understanding the Bible; based upon Adam eating from the tree of knowledge of good and evil in the garden of Eden and God sacrificing Jesus on the cross as a result.

Adventist: A member of any of various Christian sects emphasizing belief in the imminent second coming of Christ.

Agnostic: A person who claims neither faith nor disbelief in God.

Anabaptist: A Christian movement that traces its origins to the Radical Reformation; views itself as a separate branch of Christianity.

Anglican: Associated with the Church of England following the English Reformation. Members are called Anglicans, or in some countries, Episcopalians.

Anthropomorphism: The attribution of human traits, emotions, or intentions to non-human entities. It is considered to be an innate tendency of human psychology.

Apologetics: The religious discipline of defending doctrines through systematic argumentation and discourse.

Ashram: A hermitage, monastic community, or other place of religious retreat.

Assemblies of God: A group of churches that forms the largest Pentecostal denomination existing in 190 countries. It has 375 thousand churches and 69 million members.

Atheist: A person who disbelieves or lacks belief in the existence of God.

Awareness: The state of being conscious of something. To be aware is to personally know and perceive, to feel, or to be cognizant of events.

Baptist: A Protestant Christian denomination advocating baptism of adult believers by total immersion.

Belief: Sometimes based upon verifiable knowledge and sometimes not, like with whether a person is trustworthy or not, based upon hearsay or intuition.

Bible: A collection of religious texts or scriptures sacred to Christians. It appears in the form of an anthology, a compilation of texts of a variety of formats.

Black box: A device, system or object which can be viewed in terms of its inputs and outputs, without any visibility into its internal workings.

Blasphemy: Lack of reverence concerning a deity, a sacred object, or something considered unchallengeable.

Bloodletting: The withdrawal of blood by a physician, sometimes through leeches, intended to prevent or cure illness and disease.

Blue-chip stock: A stock in a corporation with a national reputation for quality, reliability, and the ability to operate profitably in good and bad times.

Book of Mormon: A sacred text of the Latter-Day Saint movement, which, according to Latter-Day Saint theology, contains writings of ancient prophets who lived on the American continent from approximately 2200 BC to AD 421.

Buford, Bob (1939-2018): A best-selling author, successful businessperson, and influential architect who used his relationship with Peter Drucker to help create the Christian megachurch movement.

Business model: The rationale of how an organization creates, delivers, and captures value in economic, social, cultural, or other contexts.

Calvinist: An adherent of the Protestant theological system of John Calvin and his successors.

Cancel: A form of ostracism in which someone is thrust out of social or professional circles online, on social media, or in person— said to be "canceled."

Carrot and stick: Metaphor for reward and punishment to induce a desired behavior.

Catholicism: The faith, practice, and church order of the Roman Catholic Church, sometimes including the Orthodox Catholic Church.

Charismatic: A form of Christianity that emphasizes the work of the Holy Spirit, spiritual gifts, speaking in tongues, and modern-day miracles as an everyday part of a believer's life.

Christ Consciousness: A believed awareness of a higher self as part of a universal system, common concept among many different religious traditions and is not unique to Christianity.

Christian: Someone who professes to believe in Christianity.

Christian Consciousness: Being consciously aware of and responsive to oneself, one's Christian faith, and one's surroundings in a loving way.

Christianity: The Christian religion.

Christianity, Inc. (Incorporated): The collection of organizations that produce the Christian ecosystem.

Christian Nationalism: Christianity-affiliated nationalism, primarily focused on passing laws that reflect their view of Christianity and its role in political and social life.

Christian Snapshot™: A survey and report that synthesizes people's beliefs for themselves and designated peer group(s); used to inform the deconstruction process.

Closed System: A business that operates an open system interacts with its environment. In a closed system, interactions are shut off from the outside world and limits the organization's ability to learn and grow.

Collins, Jim (James C.) (b. 1958): Best-selling author and management guru in the business and social sectors, including education, healthcare, government, faith-based organizations, social ventures, and cause-driven nonprofits.

Communicator: One of the major innovations of the megachurch in the 20th century, separating the evangelistically professional "communicator" from traditional pastoral duties, able to be broadcast across multi-site churches via the use of technology.

Confederate: Group officially in existence from February 8, 1861, to May 9, 1865; fought against the United States during the American Civil War.

Connotation: A commonly understood cultural or emotional association that any given word or phrase carries, in addition to its explicit or literal meaning.

Conscious: To be fully aware of something, as it truly exists, through unobstructed, direct experience.

Conscious Christianity: The practice of Christianity which focuses on Jesus' priorities, with the Bible embraced as a remarkable history of the Judeo-Christian tradition, without requiring literal interpretations of unprovable dogma in or outside the Bible.

Conscious Christian: Someone who practices Christianity without dogma.

Constantine (c. 272–337): Roman emperor from 306 to 337 AD; also known as Constantine the Great.

Consultant: An independent party that helps organizations analyze and improve their performance.

Contemplative: In Christianity, contemplation refers to a content-free mind directed towards the awareness of God as a living reality.

Cross the line: To go beyond what is proper or acceptable.

Crusades: Christian campaigns held in the 13th century with the objective of conquering the Holy Land from Islamic rule. Millions of deaths resulted.

Deconstruction: An overarching process of questioning core beliefs; literally meaning to break down and analyze something to discover its true significance.

Dianetics: A book about the metaphysical relationship between the mind and body published in 1950 by L. Ron Hubbard. Its principles are practiced by followers of Scientology.

Disorienting dilemma: Occurs when an individual is provided with or experiences disconfirming evidence that offers an alternative perspective and causes the individual to question deeply held beliefs.

Doctrine: A body of teachings or instructions, taught principles, or positions, as in a given branch of knowledge or belief system.

Dogma: Beliefs that are not provable by outside parties and imposed as unquestionably true by an organization's leaders.

Double down: Strengthen one's commitment to a strategy or course of action, typically one that is potentially risky.

Drucker, Peter: Management consultant, educator, and author, whose writings contributed to the philosophical and practical foundations of the modern business corporation and megachurch.

Duality: Two things are separate or opposite, like the heads and tails of a coin. Dualistic thinking produces information through separation.

Ecosystem: A complex network or interconnected system.

Enneagram: A personality instrument that describes patterns in how people interpret the world and manage their emotions.

Edict of Milan: A proclamation that permanently established religious toleration for Christianity within the Roman Empire between the Roman emperors Constantine I and Licinius in February 313 AD.

Episcopal: Describes itself as "Protestant, yet Catholic;" claims apostolic succession; traces its bishops back to the apostles via holy orders.

Evangelical: Christian group that believes the Bible is the inerrant word of God and embraces an Adam-based theology emphasizing salvation by faith in the atoning death of Jesus Christ; emphasizes the importance of preaching instead of ritual.

Feucht, Sean (b. 1983): Christian singer, songwriter, and worship leader. In 2020, Feucht ran as a Republican for congress in California's 3rd congressional district.

Flagellation: The practice of whipping used for medicinal purposes; first recorded around 25 BC.

Francis of Assisi (1181 or 1182–1226): 12th-century Italian mystic; canonized in 1228 by Pope Gregory IX.

Fundamentalist: Firm believer that the Bible came from God and is to be interpreted literally. Religious militants in direct opposition to secularization.

Gaslighting: Manipulating victims psychologically by questioning their sanity, such as when telling deconstructing Christians that they were never true Christians.

God: A power greater than ourselves. Viewed in different ways by Christians, God in the Bible is personified as the great *I Am*, love, and spirit.

Godhead: The divinity or substance of the Christian God, especially as existing in three persons—the Father, Son, and Holy Spirit.

Gospels: The first four books of the New Testament: Matthew, Mark, Luke, and John.

Hard-wired: A function that is a permanent feature in a computer by means of permanently connected circuits, so that it cannot be altered by software.

Hippocrates (c. 460 to c. 370 BC): Considered the father of medicine, he lived in ancient Greece.

Heresy: A belief or theory strongly at variance with established beliefs or customs, in particular the accepted beliefs of a church or religious organization.

Holon: Something that is simultaneously a whole in and of itself, as well as a part of a larger whole.

Holy Spirit: The third person of the Godhead for the majority of Christian denominations. Also referred to as the Holy Ghost.

Homophobia: A dualistic, heterosexual fear of and subsequent marginalization of people who are identified or perceived as being lesbian, gay, bisexual, transgender, and queer.

Hubbard, L. Ron (1911–1986): American science fiction author; founded the Church of Scientology.

In cahoots: An alliance or partnership. In most contexts, it describes the conspiring activity of people up to no good.

Independent Christian: Not a denomination, per se, but a group of autonomous churches with no central headquarters.

Innovation: The creation of a new product, process, or service.

Interdependency: Dependence between things, often used to describe complex systems.

Islam: The world's second-largest religion with 1.9 billion followers, known as Muslims, who regard Muhammad (c. 570–632 AD) as God's messenger.

Jesus Christ: The central figure of the Christian religion, who prioritized love over law and was the personification of divinity and humanity.

Jesus-centric theology: A theological model for understanding the Bible based upon what Jesus said was most important: love, connection, and service.

"Jesus wept": Famous for being the shortest verse in the Bible; found in John 11:35.

John the Baptist: Jewish mystic from the first century considered the forerunner of Jesus; executed via decapitation by Herod Antipas (c. 30 AD).

Ku Klux Klan: Commonly shortened to the KKK or the Klan. American white supremacist terrorist hate group whose primary targets are African Americans as well as Jews, immigrants, leftists, homosexuals, Catholics, and Muslims.

Lamb: In Christianity, the lamb symbolizes sacrifice, gentleness, innocence, sweetness, forgiveness, meekness, and purity.

Levites: The Jewish clerical class in the Old Testament; served as teachers and judges, maintained cities of refuge in biblical times.

Lewis, C.S. (1898–1963): A British novelist, poet, academic, medievalist, literary critic, essayist, lay theologian, broadcaster, lecturer, and Christian apologist.

Liberal Christianity: A movement that interprets and reforms Christian teaching by emphasizing the importance of reason and experience over doctrinal authority.

Luther, Martin (1483–1546): A German professor of theology, priest, author, composer, Augustinian monk, and a seminal figure in the Reformation in the 16th century.

Lutheran: One of the largest branches of Protestantism; identifies with the teachings of Martin Luther.

Knowledge: Something that is known and can be proven by outsiders.

McDowell, Josh (b. 1939): American Christian apologist, evangelist, and writer. He is within the Evangelical tradition of Protestant Christianity and is the author or co-author of more than 100 books.

McDowell, Sean (b. 1976): Associate professor in the Christian Apologetics program at Talbot School of Theology, Biola University (La Mirada, CA); son of apologist Josh McDowell.

Meditative prayer: The integrative practice of mindfulness meditation combined with the conscious Christian priorities of love, connection, and service.

Megachurch: A church with a large membership, professional communicator, and highly developed technology; usually Protestant or Evangelical.

Meta-dogma: Dogma used to explain other dogma.

Metaphysical: An idea, doctrine, or posited reality outside of human sense perception, including studies of things beyond objective material reality.

Methodist: Christian Protestant denomination originating in the 18th-century evangelistic movement of Charles and John Wesley and George Whitefield.

Military-industrial complex: Refers to an informal alliance between a nation's military and the defense industry that supplies it, seen together as a vested interest that influences public policy.

Mindfulness meditation: A practice to improve personal consciousness through building the capability to maintain a moment-by-moment awareness of thoughts, feelings, and sensations through a loving and nurturing lens.

Misogyny: The hatred of, contempt for, marginalization of, and/or prejudice against women or girls.

Muhammad (570–632 AD): An Arab religious, social, and political leader; the founder of Islam.

Mystic: A person who seeks by contemplation and self-surrender to obtain unity with or absorption into the absolute or believes in the spiritual apprehension of truths beyond the intellect.

Natural Selection: The theoretical process whereby organisms that better adapt to their environment tend to survive and produce more offspring.

New Age: A contemporary cultural movement concerned with spiritual consciousness; its adherents variously combine dogmatic beliefs (i.e., reincarnation and astrology).

NIV: The New International Version is an English translation of the Bible first published in 1978 by Biblica.

Non-duality: (n) Rather than being separate, like the heads and tails of a coin, something is connected and whole and part of a bigger picture, like the coin itself. Non-dualistic thinking produces meaning through connection.

NXIVM: An American multi-level marketing company and cult that engaged in sex trafficking, forced labor and racketeering, recruiting members by offering personal and professional development seminars.

Omnipotence: The quality of having unlimited power and potential.

Omnipresence: The ability to be present everywhere at the same time.

Omniscience: The state of knowing everything.

Organization: An entity that functions as a group to achieve outcomes that cannot be achieved through individuals.

Organizational hierarchy: The power structure of an organization, defining who has authority over what. The hierarchy ultimately has a single point of organizational control.

Organizational governance: The oversight of the organizational power structure intended to ensure that leaders are performing their duties and not abusing their power.

Panpsychism: Theory that the mind is a fundamental feature of the world which exists throughout the universe.

Paradigm shift: A fundamental change in approach or underlying assumptions.

Paul (c. 5–64/67 AD): The Apostle Paul. His letters to early Christians make up nearly 30% of the New Testament.

Pentecostal: Christian movements and individuals emphasizing baptism in the Holy Spirit, evidenced by speaking in tongues, prophecy, healing, and exorcism.

Perks: Special benefits given to people with a particular job or who belong to a particular group.

Pharisees: Members of a party who believed in resurrection and following legal traditions that were ascribed to "the traditions of the fathers."

Platform: An environment for building and running applications, systems, and processes viewed as toolsets for developing and operating customized and tailored services.

Post-modernism: Philosophical movement of relativism, largely a reaction to the modernistic certainty of scientific, or objective, efforts to explain reality.

Practitioner: A person actively engaged in an art, discipline, or profession on a day-to-day basis, such as a manager in a company or a minister in a church.

Presbyterian: Belonging or relating to a Protestant church, found mainly in Scotland or the United States, which is governed by a body of official people of equal rank.

Protestantism: A form of Christianity that originated with the 16th-century Reformation.

Quaker: A member of the Religious Society of Friends, a Christian movement founded by George Fox in the 17th century, focused on peaceful principles.

Quran: The central religious text of Islam, believed by Muslims to be a revelation from God.

Racism: A dualistically-based belief in the inherent superiority of a race that leads to marginalizing of groups of humans based on their race or ethnicity.

Reformation: A movement within Western Christianity in 16th-century Europe that posed a religious and political challenge to Catholicism and the authority of the Pope.

Religion: A system of faith and worship.

Right wing: The conservative or reactionary section of a political party or system.

Root cause analysis: A method of problem-solving used for identifying the root causes of faults or problems.

Rorschach test: Examines a person's personality characteristics and emotional functioning.

Sadducees: Members of a Jewish sect that denied the resurrection of the dead, the existence of spirits, and emphasized acceptance of the written Law alone.

Scaling: Setting the stage to enable and support growth without being hampered. It requires planning, funding, systems, staff, processes, technology, and partners.

Schaeffer, Francis A. (1912–1984): American Evangelical theologian, apologist, philosopher, and Presbyterian pastor; author of book and video series, *How Should We Then Live? The Rise and Decline of Western Thought and Culture.*

Sermon on the Mount: The longest conversation from Jesus found in the New Testament. It includes some of his best-known teachings, such as the Beatitudes and the Lord's Prayer.

Seven wonders of the world: Great pyramid of Giza, the Hanging Gardens of Babylon, the Statue of Zeus at Olympia, Greece, the Temple of Artemis at Ephesus, the Mausoleum at Halicarnassus, the Colossus of Rhodes, and the Lighthouse of Alexandria, Egypt.

Sin: An unconscious thought or act that causes pain to yourself and others.

Smith, Joseph (1806–1844): American religious leader; author of the *Book of Mormon*; founder of Mormonism and the Latter-Day Saint movement.

Socialite: A Christian who plays along but primarily joins the church for social reasons.

Southern Baptist: A large convention of Baptist churches established in the US in 1845, typically having a fundamentalist and evangelistic approach to Christianity.

Speaking in tongues: A practice in which people utter words or speech-like sounds, often thought by believers to be languages unknown to the speaker.

Spiritual but not religious: A life stance that does not regard organized religion as the sole or most valuable means of furthering spiritual growth.

Spirituality: A belief in and practice of loving selflessness, often embracing that which is greater than oneself.

Theologian: Someone who systematically studies the nature of religious beliefs. Theology is taught as an academic discipline, typically in universities and seminaries.

Tetragrammaton: The four-letter Hebrew word YHWH and name of the biblical god of Israel.

Thomas Merton (1915–1968): American mystic and Trappist monk.

Thirty Years' War: A conflict fought in Europe from 1618 to 1648 between Catholics and Protestants with an estimated death toll of more than 5 million people.

Thought experiment: An imaginary situation in which a hypothesis, theory, or principle is laid out for the purpose of thinking through its consequences.

Transformation: The transmutation, metamorphosis, or reconstruction of one thing into another.

Trinity: The non-dualistic doctrine that God is the Father, the Son, and the Holy Spirit. The three persons are distinct, yet are one substance, essence, or nature.

Truth: Something that is believed based upon verifiable knowledge.

Tweet: A tweet is a post on Twitter. The act of writing a tweet is called tweeting or twittering. Tweets can be up to 140 characters long.

Unconscious: To be unaware of something as it truly exists; to be lost in thought, unable to think, or constrained by preconceived biases.

Yahweh: Before the term God was used, YHWH, the god of the Israelites, was used. The term was given by Moses as four Hebrew letters called the tetragrammaton. The meaning of the name Yahweh has been interpreted as "He Who Makes That Which Has Been Made" or "He Brings Into Existence Whatever Exists."

White supremacist: Believes that white people constitute a superior race and should therefore dominate society over all other races.

Word of knowledge: Proclaiming that one's thought comes directly from God; linked to 1 Corinthians 12:8, NLT: "To one person the Spirit gives the ability to give wise advice; to another the same Spirit gives a message of special knowledge."

Wishy-washy: Feeble or insipid in quality or character; lacking strength or boldness.

Xenophobia: The dualistic fear and hatred of strangers or foreigners or of anything strange or foreign.

Zacharias, Ravi (1946–2020): Conservative Christian apologist over a forty-year period, founder of Ravi Zacharias International Ministries (RZIM), and author of more than 30 books.

Acknowledgments

DURING THE RESEARCH for and writing of this book I integrated thousands of thoughts and experiences. Some were my own and many came from others. While the acknowledgements are incomplete, and are not endorsements for or from anyone involved, a very eclectic group of people and organizations over a period of many years have influenced my thinking and helped to make this book possible.

Most directly, I would like to thank Rachel L. Hall, who was my writing partner and editor. With the manuscript itself, I'd like to thank a variety of people who provided critical feedback. I'd especially like to thank Phil Drysdale of the Deconstruction Network, who generously helped me in many ways. David Gushee, the Christian ethicist, pastor, author, and advocate, helped me through his many books, manuscript critique, and personal advice. Bart Campolo, the founder of Humanize Me and previous Evangelical leader, provided invaluable feedback, educating me via his own journey. Joshua Harris was also very helpful, providing invaluable insights about the manuscript, his life's journey from Purity Culture icon and megachurch pastor to a publicly deconstructing figure actively trying to help others. His personal coaching greatly helped me to better understand both the current evangelical and deconstruction landscapes. My children, Ted and Rachel Bergstrand, provided important perspectives, as did my friends Tom Miller,

Dorothy Vollmer, Katie Arabis, and Alan Kisling. Dorothy Vollmer helped immensely with operationalizing the Christian Snapshot.

Indirectly, as I synthesized the contents in this book, I was influenced by many people and groups. Influence here also does not equate to agreement by either side but was nevertheless very important to me. People and groups who influenced my thinking included my childhood pastor Donald Ortlund, Robert H. Schuller, Bob Buford, the Halftime Institute, the Leadership Network, Tom McGehee, Jo Luehmann, Dino Robusto, Josh McDowell, C.S. Lewis, Francis Schaeffer, Meghan O'Gieblyn, Katherine Stewart, Richard Rohr, Gil Fronsdal, Rachel Held Evans, Eckhart Tolle, Sam Harris, Andy Stanley and North Point Ministries, Peter Enns, Humanize Me, Tim Whitaker and the New Evangelicals, The Deconstruction Network, Brad Onishi and the *Straight White American Jesus* podcast, Blake Chastain's *Exvangelical* podcast. Rob Bell, William MacAskill, John Shelby Spong, Advashanti, Annaka Harris, Wayne Dyer, Thomas Merton, Lloyd Reeb, and my ChristianConsciousnessOrg Instagram friends.

Another source of influence with how this book was conceptualized and written was from my experience as a business executive and business transformation consultant, affected by my work and education in business, consulting, and the social sciences. Large influences were my two decades working in the global Coca-Cola system, two decades working with Consequent clients, my education at Stanford Business School, George Washington University, and Michigan State, my association with the Drucker Institute, and many insights from the works of Peter Drucker, Roger Martin, Jim Collins, and Peter Senge.

At the most basic level, I'm sure I would not have even been interested in this subject at this stage of my life were it not for several strong influences during my formative years. Evangelicalism was a major part of my upbringing, and even though it had plenty of dogma and was influenced almost exclusively by straight white males, the Evangelical church seemed a lot less militant a half-century ago. My experience as an Evangelical was mainly oriented around Jesus, love, non-judgment, forgiveness, and helping people. I grew up in a conservative, loving, and upright Christian home, and I spent a lot of time at the

Homewood Evangelical Free Church in Moline, Illinois, and the Timber-Lee Christian Center in East Troy, Wisconsin. During my youth, many high-integrity Evangelical leaders and friends helped me, and I appreciate them to this day.

Most importantly, I would like to thank my wife Xin (Cynthia) Jiang, who provided me the space and encouragement to synthesize my Christian belief system while I was writing this book. Cyn, you fill my soul in the most special way, and I love you completely.

About the Author

JACK BERGSTRAND IS a business transformation consultant and Christian deconstruction observer. He wrote *Christianity without Dogma* to try to help Christians by using his perspective as a consultant to independently deconstruct Christianity as a system, including how it works, why it works the way it does, and how it could potentially be reinvented in a more Jesus-centric way.

Jack spent 20 years as a business executive for The Coca-Cola Company. His last position there was as the company's chief information officer. He left Coke and founded a business transformation consulting firm on his 43rd birthday, Consequent (cnsqnt.com), which has worked with many large companies over the past 20 years.

Jack's work on *Christianity without Dogma*, ChristianConsciousness. org, and ChristianSnapshot.com was done to help provide deconstructing Christians with a more systematic way to think about and potentially reinvent their Christian faiths.

Jack lives in Atlanta, Georgia, with his wife, Cynthia. and has two adult children, Ted and Rachel. He is a self-described "conscious Christian," and has worked extensively with large commercial enterprises, in the social sector, and with technology entrepreneurs over the past 40 years. He has master's degrees in education, management, and advertising from George Washington, Stanford, and Michigan State Universities.

Previous books include *Reinvent Your Enterprise* and *The Velocity Advantage*.

Index

Note: Page numbers in italics indicate figures or tables.

Jack can be reached via:

Instagram: @ChristianConsciousnessOrg
Website: ChristianConsciousness.org
Address: P.O. Box 191925; Atlanta, GA. 31119

Made in the USA
Las Vegas, NV
16 August 2023